To Mark,

With best wishes

for your "research"!

Love,

Eleanor

# With A Song In My Heart

Eleanor W. Moylan

iUniverse, Inc.
New York   Bloomington
*In Association with Bilbo Books*

iUniverse books may be ordered through booksellers or by contacting:

iUniverse
1663 Liberty Drive
Bloomington, IN 47403
www.iuniverse.com
1-800-Authors (1-800-288-4677)

Because of the dynamic nature of the Internet, any Web addresses or links contained in this book may have changed since publication and may no longer be valid. The views expressed in this work are solely those of the author and do not necessarily reflect the views of the publisher, and the publisher hereby disclaims any responsibility for them.

ISBN: 978-1-4502-0715-7 (sc)
ISBN: 978-1-4502-0716-4 (ebook)

Printed in the United States of America

iUniverse rev. date: 04/05/2010

Cover design by Isabell VanMerlin
**Author's picture by Brett Turner Photography**

A well-composed book is a magic carpet on which we are wafted to a world we cannot enter in any other way. – Caroline Gordon

# Table of Contents

My Father ............................................................................... 1
My Mother ............................................................................... 9
My Life ................................................................................... 15
My Life—High School ........................................................... 22
Meeting My Future ................................................................ 26
Richmond Days ..................................................................... 30
First Pastorate ...................................................................... 35
Second Pastorate ................................................................. 40
Pastorate Revisited .............................................................. 44
Extended Ministery .............................................................. 49
Sailing Adventures ............................................................... 56
Oldfield Road House ............................................................ 60
Summer Travels ................................................................... 66
Holiday Adventures .............................................................. 73
Turbulent Times ................................................................... 78
Overseas Teaching .............................................................. 82
Overseas Teaching 1984 ..................................................... 89
Reconciliation ....................................................................... 99
Dog Days ............................................................................ 103
David's Death ..................................................................... 107
Asheville Move .................................................................... 113
New Partner ........................................................................ 125
Rainbow Ridge .................................................................... 138
Faraway Adventures ........................................................... 151
Chunn's View ...................................................................... 162
South to Athens .................................................................. 175
Last House .......................................................................... 185
Backward Glance ................................................................ 192
Appendix A (genealogy) ...................................................... 203

To my mother and father

# ACKNOWLEDGEMENTS

I would like to thank my friends from as far north as Maine and as far south as Ecuador, South America, who gave me invaluable help on dates and places as well as experiences.

My doctors, therapists, church members, and instructors who have helped me keep body and soul strong during the writing of my autobiography.

My family who will be happy not to have every conversation start with, "Do you remember_____--_____?" Especially my granddaughter, Hannah, who unraveled all of the mysteries of the computer program I used.

To the Iris Place Retirement Community, whose residents and staff showed concern for my problems and rejoiced with me at any good news. This was apparent on a daily basis and they are a living testimony to "gracious living."

To my publishers, Bilbo Books, who took on the herculean task of editing, encouraging, and overseeing a first-time author. Their vision for the book kept me going. I am particularly grateful for their thoroughness through every phase of the book.

Last, but not least, my husband, Tom, who filled in as "chief cook and bottle washer" as well as secretary, keeping my time free to write.

---

# PROLOGUE

The date was November 9, 1620. At daybreak, the passengers and crew of the Mayflower sighted a shore which had wooded land right to the edge of the beach. A cheer arose from the deck, for after sixty-five days on the North Atlantic, these weary pilgrims were ready to feel ground beneath their feet.

Among the passengers were William Bradford, who was to become Plymouth, Massachusetts' first governor, Myles Standish, chosen to lead a military regiment, and John Alden, who was twenty-one. He was a cooper by trade. These same names are also found in my family's genealogy.

Eight generations later, my mother's father, Evans Shipman Kellogg, was born in Lansing, New York, in 1876. His parents were Charles Harvey Kellogg and Frances Amelia Parmelee. John Alden was at the beginning of his paternal line. William Bradford and Myles Standish were at the beginning of his maternal line.

My grandfather, Evans Shipman Kellogg, was married to my grandmother, Cornelia Helen Mather, at her parents' home in Stamford, Connecticut. The announcement appeared in the New York Times on May 13<sup>th</sup>, 1906.   The heading read, KELLOGG-MATHER WEDDING – *Veil Handed Down from Theodore Roosevelt's Grandmother Worn by Bride. This famous wedding veil, was given by Mrs. Roosevelt, grandmother of the President, to Mrs. John M. Olcott, the bride's grandmother, at the time of the latter's wedding.* The veil was made of Brusssels lace.

My mother, Emily Mather Kellogg, was born in 1907, and was the only child of my grandparents. It was a lonesome childhood with no siblings.

# CHAPTER 1

My father, William Scott Whiting, Jr., was the fourth child and second son of William Scott Whiting and Caroline Lorentz Link.

The earliest family history of my father shows that the Reverend Samuel Whiting came to Saugus, Massachusetts, in 1636. Here he was installed as the minister of a little church there. He was born in Boston, England, and had been the rector of St. Margaret's Church in Lynn Regis, England. But because of his non-conformist ideas, he felt Massachusetts would be more accepting of his beliefs. With him came his second wife, who was the daughter of Oliver St. John – a cousin of Oliver Cromwell. Massachusetts honored Rev. Whiting by changing the town's name of Saugus to Lynn. Seven generations later, John Whiting moved to Maine after he had married. Their son, Henry, moved to the Upper Peninsula of Northern Michigan. Here they settled in a small town on the St. Clair River.

My grandfather, William Scott Whiting, who was their youngest son, was born in 1871. Having been introduced to the lumber business by an uncle in the same area, he traveled south, to pursue the possibilities of starting a lumber business in North Carolina, several years after graduating from the University of Michigan in Ann Arbor.  He arrived in Lenoir, North Carolina, and met my grandmother, Caroline Lorentz Link.  Her father, the postmaster of Lenoir, would not let them marry for five years, because he had come from Michigan - and Yankees were viewed with suspicion!  My grandmother, an accomplished pianist, was the first female organist in western North Carolina.  She had graduated from a female seminary in Tennessee (as women's colleges were called in that day).

Soon after my father was born on April 11, 1907, in Abingdon, Virginia, the family moved to Asheville, North Carolina, where they resided in a large two-story shingled house on Montford Avenue (The house is still standing).  His father was a very successful lumberman.  He would buy or lease thousands of acres of land for the lumber and the building of lumber mills in North Carolina and Tennessee.

In 1920, the family moved to Shulls Mills, North Carolina - just south of Blowing Rock.  There his father built a large estate with farmland, barns, and a caretaker's house.  At that time my father and his older brother, Henry, rode the train back to Asheville to attend Asheville School for Boys - which is still a well-known private school in Asheville.  During the five years my father attended this school, he was captain of the soccer team, played violin in the school orchestra, and made beautiful wood carvings in the woodworking shop.  One of these carvings is a thirteen by eleven inch picture frame which holds a formal setting of his mother and her four children, made in 1912 by the studio of N. Brock of Asheville.  This picture sits today in my bookcase – a reminder of one of his many talents.

The summer after my father graduated from Asheville School for Boys in 1925, my grandfather drove him to Charleston, South Carolina, where he worked his way over to Germany on a cargo ship.  His love for the violin inspired him to go there to buy a fine violin. While he was there, he also bought a handsome guitar with mother-of-pearl inlaid around the sides. In the fall, he entered Rensselaer Polytechnic Institute where he majored in mechanical engineering. During his senior year, he met my mother, Emily Kellogg, and they were married before he returned home to North Carolina in 1929.

In the summer between his junior and senior years in college, my father converted his Model T Ford to fit the railroad tracks of the logging railroad between Butler, Tennessee, and Beech Mountain, North Carolina. On one occasion, my father was riding down the railroad tracks in his car, when suddenly he realized a train was coming. This was a logging train pulling lumber from Beech Mountain. He sped up, quickly looking for a crossing onto which he got the Ford off the tracks. That is what I would say was a "close call." I have never heard if he ever tried this again!

My father's first job was in a lumber mill in Butler, Tennessee, which belonged to his father. He was fortunate to find a job during these years of the Depression. Soon after I was born in 1931, we moved to Canton, North Carolina, where he had been hired by Champion Paper and Fiber Company. The large house on Fiberville Hill met all the needs of this growing family.

Having a brilliant mind, he was twenty-three when he was awarded his first patent for an automatic toaster. This toaster measured about eight inches across, twelve inches high, and deep enough to hold eight pieces of bread. The bread rotated on a small-wheeled pulley system past a heating unit, dropping to counter level as toast. My younger brother remembers this toaster! My father received nine patents in all, one of which was awarded to him after his death. This last invention was for a hand barrow which would fold up when not in use, and the drawing shows it to be about the height and size of our grocery carts.

Music had always been a part of my father's life. His mother, an accomplished pianist, had provided music in the home from the time he was born. His older sister, Anna Belle, studied piano at the Curtis Institute of Music in Philadelphia, Pennsylvania. Upon returning to Asheville when she married, Anna Belle would often play at social events. My father's older brother, Henry, kept music going in his married life as a member of the Detroit, Michigan, Barbershop Quartet.

As we grew to the age to be able to learn a musical instrument, my older sister, Cornelia, began violin lessons at age nine. I followed with the flute at age eight. My younger sister, Mary Rice, started piano lessons at age five! Sunday afternoons in our house were reserved for playing music as a group, which was rounded out with my cello-playing mother. My father was very proud of his family orchestra! Until I left for college, any one of this family group who was still at home was found around the piano on Sunday afternoons. Cornelia played violin for many years. The last time I heard her play was the duet we performed at my brother's second wedding in 1988. Mary Rice still plays the piano. On one memorable occasion, she was complimented by the judge when I received a superior rating in flute competition my senior year of high school. I am convinced my performance was enhanced by her accompaniment. After Mary Rice married and became the proud mother of six fine boys, each son was encouraged to learn to play the piano. I played my flute until the arthritis in my left hand made it impossible to reach all the keys.

My father taught my two sisters and me how to use every tool correctly in his tool box. I still wonder if he was afraid there were going to be no boys, or whether he wanted us to be prepared to handle jobs needing these tools after we left home.

In 1941, the family moved to Hartsville, South Carolina, where my father was employed as an engineer for Sonoco

Products Company. He designed and had built a lovely two-story house with white asbestos shingles and yellow blinds. A huge playroom with a fireplace, bathroom, and a small apartment filled the basement. I was very happy during the seven years I lived there. These were my "growing-up" years.

Physically, my mother could not tolerate the South Carolina heat, so my father built a cabin on land owned by his parents eleven miles south of Blowing Rock, North Carolina. He designed a pump to bring water from an artesian spring on the riverbank just below the cabin site. It was still useable when the property was sold in 1980.

During the building of this cabin, my father took my two sisters and me overnight camping on the hillside below the cabin site. We were warm in the tent and sleeping soundly, until I awoke to see a big brown bear just below the tent, enjoying the bacon we had brought for breakfast! My father came to the rescue, banging on the frying pan, and we ate what was left.

My father began his flying career in Hartsville, taking lessons at the "air strip" on the edge of town. At this time he was flying a Sky Ranger which he unfortunately crashed near the airstrip. He was fine, but my younger sister has a scar on her lip today from biting through it upon impact.

This small airport held mixed memories for me. When I was learning to drive, my father would take me with him. While he was in the air, flying for recreation, I would drive the family car around the air strip. One Sunday afternoon, I felt that I was confident enough to try the adjoining dirt road leading to a nearby farm. I had not gone very far, when one of the wheels got stuck in a deep rut in the road. Walking to the farm, I told the farmer what I needed. He obligingly brought his tractor over and pulled me out. Thanking him profusely, I returned to the air strip just as my father was landing his plane. When he came to the car where I was waiting, he laughingly said, "Well, I see you had a little trouble on the road." He had seen the whole affair from his plane above me!

Any time he was able to fly, my father was happy! On the weekends during the summer, he would fly to our cabin in North Carolina to spend time with my mother and us. My grandmother had sold several acres to the Blue Ridge Parkway Association for the completion of the parkway. Since this land adjoined our cabin property, it was very convenient for him to land on this ungraded part. One weekend in the summer of 1952, he joined the family on Friday evening. Monday morning, he prepared to fly back to home and, to his surprise, there was a ticket on his windshield – stating that he was illegally parked! I never heard the outcome of that story.

In 1948, my father moved our family to Camden, South Carolina. Here he began Whiting Products. After working for two companies for seventeen years, he felt ready to create his own designs. He would visit textile mills in the southwestern part of the state. Here he would see what machines were being used and design a machine that would save time and labor. The machine would be manufactured at his plant in Camden and transported to the mills. After making sure the machine was satisfactory - he would repeat this process, making enough money to support our family. Most of the mills my father visited were southwest of Columbia, our state capital. He even invented a fold-up motorbike, to give him quicker access to the plant he was visiting. Sometimes, on returning from trips to these mills, the weather would be foggy. After his death, friends would tell the family how they could hear his plane flying low beneath the clouds above the highway between the two towns.

I had the unfortunate problem of throwing up whenever I was flying with him. Although he enjoyed taking me on flights around the state, I would never throw up until the airport was in sight and he had begun his descent.  On the last occasion I that I flew with my father, he offered to fly me to Savannah, Georgia, where I was to be in a friend's wedding.  I was nineteen at the time. We lifted off from the Camden airport on a beautiful June afternoon.  As soon as we were airborne, he turned to me and said, "Now, you are going to fly to Savannah. I will tell you what to do." Being a dual control plane, this made sense only to him. Well, I did it and fortunately can't remember how - except that I was so scared, I forgot to throw up when the Savannah Airport came into view and he took over the controls.  My friend who met me at the airport did not comment on my "pale" face!

Being active in the Kiwanis Club of Camden, my father was asked to represent Camden at the national convention in Seattle, Washington.  This assignment he happily accepted – another chance to fly!  My brother, Evans, was fourteen at the time and he joined him on this trip in the summer of 1951. They left Camden, flying west along the northern part of the United States until they reached Seattle.  After the convention, my father and brother flew south along the California coast, turning eastward to return home, the southern route.  My brother developed a love for flying.  His thirty years of flying for Northwest Airlines brought him a lifetime of adventure. My father would drive to our cabin in North Carolina to spend the weekends with my mother.  Getting tired of the winding mountain roads the last hour, he decided to have an airstrip built on the property in back of the cabin.  This took several summers to complete.  Finally, the last inspection was made by the road commissioner, so he happily left on the first Saturday afternoon of April, 1957, to fly to Lenoir, North Carolina.

The Lenoir airport had been built recently and not all of the telephone poles had been erected.  There was an order for this to be done on the following Monday. As my father descended onto the landing strip, a telephone wire on the approach was hidden by the roof line of a house on the opposite side of the field. The wing of his recently purchased Piper Tri Pacer caught on the wire.  The plane crashed and burned at the edge of the field. My mother received the call from Lenoir late that night. The stranger's voice on the other end told her of my father's crash.

When I attended my father's funeral the next week, I met Henry, one of my first cousins, for the first time.  My father had one brother who had married and lived near Detroit all of his adult life. So Uncle Henry's children were the only first cousins we had.  He lived in the Detroit area.  His one sister, Beverly, was the only one I had kept in contact with through the years. We would meet at the airport when I would fly through Detroit, or I would spend several days with her after her husband had died and her children were married.  But I have always felt sad when I see my children and their cousins have such a good time together.  Beverly died several years ago, so now I have only occasional contact with any of the Michigan cousins.

# CHAPTER 2

My mother was born Emily Mather Kellogg on September 28, 1907, the only child of Evans Shipman Kellogg and Cornelia Helen Mather. It was a long time family joke that her birthplace was Schenectady, New York, and the family moved to Syracuse, NY, because my mother could not spell "Schenectady"!

Being an only child was always a burden to my mother. Because of their religious beliefs, her parents refused to let her go horseback riding with her close friends on Sundays. I am sure there were other specific reasons, but this was the only one I can remember! My mother was so definite about this burden that she strongly objected to our dating only children, and the thought of our marrying one was definitely out of the picture! (Fortunately, my three sisters and I did not encounter this problem when the time came for us to marry!)

My mother was educated at one of the best private girl's schools on the east coast - Emma Willard School in Troy, New York. My grandfather's job was in Troy at the time my mother was old enough to enter kindergarten. She attended this school until she graduated from high school.

During our growing up years four through eight, my mother tried her best to teach us French, claiming that every well educated young lady should learn to speak this language. At mealtime, we would have one day during which we were to speak only French. My older sister gallantly did so, but my younger sister and I would signal each other under the table, as to what we needed passed during the meal. Two pats on the knee meant "Please pass the butter," and one pat on the knee would mean, "Please pass the sugar."

As an adult, my mother stood erect at 5' 7". Her dark brown, fine, shoulder-length and loosely curled hair framed a heart-shaped face. The clear china blue eyes were under dark brown eyebrows and above a slim straight nose, complimenting a wide smile which revealed even teeth. My mother's slim and shapely figure never changed until she was sixty-five. I was fortunate to inherit her build. As a result, my favorite clothes were still a good fit for many years – not that they lasted that long.

Her education continued at Northwestern University in Evanston, Illinois. She wanted to major in journalism, and did well in this area for a year and a half. At that time, my grandfather changed his job location from Evanston, to return to Troy, New York, where he opened a small savings and loan company. He could not afford the expense at Northwestern; so my mother returned to Troy. Here my mother met my father, who was a mechanical engineering student at Rennsaeler Polytechnic Institute in Troy. The occasion was a fraternity dance and I guess I should say - the rest is history!

My grandfather had built a beautiful two-story house with white board siding and green shutters on a lovely street in one of the better neighborhoods in Troy. When my mother and father eloped after graduation, the event broke my grandparents' hearts. The house would have been perfect for a wedding reception. Being loving and forgiving parents, they watched their only child pack her belongings, and drive south with my father.

Here my mother lived the rest of her life - but never losing her accent or her desire for "Yankee cooking." Several times during my college vacations, I would arrive home just in time to "referee" the disagreements between our southern cooks and my mother - who insisted that green beans be steamed until "crunchy" with no seasonings.

I began lessons on the flute when I was eight. For two years, I was the youngest member of the Canton High School's marching band. We were taken to concerts at the auditorium in Asheville. One of my clearest memories was dressing up with white gloves, and going to hear Jeanette McDonald and Nelson Eddy sing "Indian Love Call."

When I was ten, my family moved to Hartsville, South Carolina, where my father was employed by Sonoco Products Company. My mother continued her research on raising healthy children – though my father complained whenever he felt that he was included in that category. He preferred the gravy and dumplings he remembered from his youth.

The large two-story house we lived in had four bedrooms and two bathrooms upstairs. Connie and I had our own rooms. Mary Rice slept with Evans, our three- year-old brother, in the third bedroom. This was a luxury because I had had to share a bedroom in Canton with my younger sister. In the full basement, my older sister would invite her friends on Friday nights to sock-hop until ten. After the boys left, the girls would sleep in sleeping bags, snacking, and talking for a long time.

The Hartsville Presbyterian Church was close enough for us to walk or ride our bicycles. Here my mother and I sang in the choir, when I became fourteen. The youth groups met on Sunday afternoons, and provided a variety of activities in which my sisters and I participated.  Our respective schools were also within a short distance.  My mother made us very independent. We made our own lunches, using whole wheat bread.  My friends at lunch time would wonder about the color of the bread! Also, we were in charge of making sure our clothes got to the laundry room.  My father had designed a chute from the second floor, into which we could throw the dirty clothes.  I remember putting the family cat down that chute several times!

Saturday was our day of accounting.  My mother had each daughter keep an account book, in which was to be listed every expense from her weekly allowance of fifty cents! If the total was not correct, we would get no allowance for the coming week. I "fixed" my expenditures so they were always correct.  This deception must have short-wired a part of my brain, because I had trouble adding and subtracting, until calculators came along.

Another ritual was morning devotionals.  We would end this in silence, and then be asked what God had told us.  I am afraid we could not come up with anything more original than not hitting our baby brother!

My mother made sure we did not have any idle moments. One of my jobs was to iron the linens on a mangle.  My long arms seemed to be suitable for this job! Even though my mother had full time help as long as she was alive to do the heavy work and cooking, she would find yard work, silver polishing, dusting, bed making, and general light tasks for us to do.  From the age of six, we girls were responsible for hand washing our socks and underwear.  The fights we would have over the upstairs bathroom sink were very loud!  My younger brother was given "manly" jobs suitable for his size.

Early afternoons on weekends and summer holidays were for napping.  My mother took naps most of her life and, until we were past the napping age, so did we. Twenty minute naps continue to "recharge" my batteries.

Having only one car which my father used to go to work, we were dependent on our bicycles and walking. This habit instilled good health from which we benefit to this day.

Hartsville was the home of Coker College, a girls' school. Here we took music lessons, and had the benefit of many cultural events. I took dancing lessons from the Sherrill School of Dance, although my large feet had a hard time with the various tap dancing routines.

When we moved to Camden, forty miles away, my mother sadly bid goodbye to our friends and a much larger house, but our new house was located on a main street quite close to the center of town. Here my mother quickly made new friends through the church and neighbors. Having never lost her New York accent, she would comment that the grocery store would always know she was ordering.

Both of my parents were helpful to people in need. Camden was asking for families to sponsor displaced persons from Russia and surrounding areas. My parents signed up for a young couple and their four-year-old son. Ignaz and Karen and their son, Jan, came to live with my parents for a year. Ignaz worked for my father in his company and Karen helped my mother with the household chores. At the end of a year, Ignaz had saved enough money to buy a small house in town and they moved there.

My mother continued her singing in the Camden Presbyterian Church choir, and was active in the meetings during the week. Upon complaining about having to go to church one Sunday, my sister asked why we had to go. My father exclaimed, "You go to worship God!"

After my father's death, my older sister and her husband and four children moved to Camden to take over my father's business. My mother continued to live in the family home until my youngest sister, Anna Belle, left for college. Mother had an income from rental property in Cleveland, Ohio. This provided for her, so that she could travel, and visit our families whenever she wished. She contracted ovarian cancer in June of 1982. Not wanting to be treated for this, she died quietly in the home of my older sister in Camden in March of 1983. On my last visit to her, I still was unable to feel close to her, grieving that we would part this way. Her words to me as I was leaving were, "Eleanor, you were my untended garden." With great sorrow, I had to agree.

# CHAPTER 3

My life began in the delivery room of the Samaritan Hospital in Troy, New York, at 8:15 a.m., on July 18, 1931. The attending doctor and nurses heard my "first song"- lusty cries! At my birth, my pioneering mother raised nurses' eyebrows by flattening one protruding ear with scotch tape. Today, my well-positioned ears attest to the fact that this idea was successful!

My parents were living in the small lumber mill town of Butler, Tennessee, at the time of my birth. There were neither doctors nor nurses available. So my mother went by train from nearby Asheville, North Carolina, to her parents' home in Troy. Six weeks after my birth, we returned to Asheville to join my father and older sister, who had also been born in Troy eighteen months before. Soon we moved to Canton, North Carolina, eighteen miles west of Asheville, where my father had been hired by Champion Paper and Fiber Company.

Our home was a large, two-story, white clapboard house with wide open porches on the front and left side. In the large side yard, there was playground equipment. The upstairs had three bedrooms and a bath. Downstairs was a gracious living room, dining room, kitchen, and back porch.

My mother was way ahead of doctors in matters of how to raise children! One example was putting us in a mattress box of which one side had been removed. This she placed in the back yard in the snow. At three months, I was put on a blanket in this box for thirty minutes around noon to receive "natural" vitamin D. The neighbors thought she was crazy!

When I was about six months old, my adoring parents heard me put together my first two words – "Come, sing." I now feel that these were a foreshadowing of my love of people and music!

As we grew, our diet reflected only the healthiest foods in my mother's opinion. I did not know that white bread existed until I saw my classmates' sandwiches when I started school. We were fed brown sugar, brown rice, and whole grain wheat. She would order brown sugar in a large wooden barrel. On passing by one afternoon, the temptation to taste the sugar overcame me, and I fell headlong into the barrel – emerging with a red face.

My father had a workshop under the front porch, where he spent many happy hours working on ideas for some inventive way to do a job better. One particular invention caused me great grief. I came down to breakfast one Saturday morning and told him, with great excitement, about my roller skating date with a close neighbor. He looked very sad, and when I questioned him, he admitted that, late the night before, as he was working in his workshop, he realized he needed one more ball bearing. My roller skate was the answer to his problem. I was one unhappy daughter!

I was playing with Pat, the next door neighbor. His mother was urging him to make his bed before we started a game. I was seven at the time, and cockily announced that I had been making my bed since I was four. His mother tried hard not to smile.

One summer, my father drove the five of us to Troy, New York, for the annual visit to my mother's parents, stopping only when necessary. One exception was made, however, when we reached Hershey, Pennsylvania. We wanted to tour the Hershey Chocolate Factory. The afternoon air smelled strongly of chocolate because of some burning of chocolate at the factory. Eagerly we began the tour by going down a long hall. On one side of the hall were attached vending machines filled with small Hershey bars. All I remember was dropping my allowance nickels into as many machines as my mother would allow. Munching on these bars kept my sisters and me quiet for many miles!

The Christmas I was six, my Whiting grandparents had invited us to spend Christmas with them at their large home in Shulls Mills, North Carolina. The main road was clear between Asheville and Shulls Mills, but the winding mountain dirt road to my grandparent's house was not passable that day. So my grandmother had Bynum, her caretaker, meet us at the main road with the horse and sleigh to take us the rest of the way. After my father parked our car in a parking lot, we transferred to the sleigh, pulling the warm lap robes over our shoulders. The horse had bells attached to his reins, which jingled merrily as we rode under the overhanging branches of fir trees laden with fresh snow. The song in my heart during the four-mile ride was, "Over the river and through the woods, to Grandmother's house we go. The horse knows the way to carry the sleigh through the white and drifting snow!"

Upon arrival, we were warmly greeted by an open fire in the stone fireplace, warm hugs from our grandparents, and pungent smells from the kitchen and the Christmas tree. My two sisters and I were put to bed early in anticipation of presents which were around the bottom of the large tree. About seven o'clock the next morning, we went down the stairs, dressed in long fluffy nightgowns, pink robes, and slippers. My mother greeted us at the bottom of the stairs. She immediately clapped her hand over her mouth exclaiming, "Eleanor, you have red spots all over your face!" My grandmother was close behind her, and confirmed that I had broken out with chicken pox during the night. Being a light case, my Christmas day was not marred. But when Ricie, my younger sister, appeared the next morning with the same red dots, my father hurriedly packed our things, and we sadly departed for home.

The next September my brother, Evans, was born. Unfortunately, Ricie and I had whooping cough at the time. So my mother had to stay with a friend until the quarantine was lifted. Sharing an upstairs bedroom which faced the street, there were two very happy faces smiling at the window when my mother opened the car door, carefully handing our brother to my father. With three older sisters to keep him happy, my parents enjoyed getting to know their first son.

My mother decided that summer camp would be beneficial the year I turned eight. Champion Paper and Fiber Company had a camp on a nearby lake. So Ricie, who was six, and I packed our warm sweaters, bathing suits, and suitable camp clothes to attend the last week in July. It was fun to swim in the clear mountain lake, and tell ghost stories after lights were out. I enjoyed the hikes the most. I had been hiking with my family on Grandfather Mountain near Blowing Rock since I was five. The cabin my father had built was three miles from the Boy Scout trail we used. The four-mile hike was complete with ladders made from logs which lifted us over the stone outcroppings.

I began my formal education when I was six. Canton was a mill town which was surrounded by low-lying foothills of the Blue Ridge Mountains. The grammar school was about a mile from our house – down a long hill, across a small river, and up another hill, to a dingy, dark red brick building with smoke darkened windows. The metal and wood desks were bolted to the dark floors on one-by- four- inch runners – very good for tripping six-year-old feet which were going too fast! My only memory of this first year was blood rolling down the aisle from where I was standing. I had previously scraped my knee. When I tripped on the wooden runner by my desk, I knocked off the scab, to the horror of my teacher!

The second grade held much happier memories. Mary Ann, a smiling curly-haired blonde with dimples was to be my roommate in my second year of college, as well as a bridesmaid in my wedding sixteen years later. The second memory was that of being kissed not once, but twice, on different occasions by Billy, a chubby round faced classmate – on the front steps of the grammar school! Many years later, at the college our middle daughter was attending, I was introduced to an outstanding mathematics professor. He smiled broadly and told me I had been his sweetheart – admitting that he was the one who had kissed me several times on the front steps of the school in the second grade!

My traveling days began very early. My grandfather's two sisters lived in the nearby town of Scotia. I had been named for one of them, and the pictures, letters, and telephone calls were not enough. So when I was seven, she drove me to Asheville to catch the overnight train for New York. She made sure I was properly seated before the train left the station. She also looked around to find the porter who would be coming to this car. Then I overheard my mother asking him if he could say my prayers before I went to sleep. When she got an affirmative answer, she paid him for this extra responsibility! My grandparents met in New York City the next day.

We moved to Hartsville in 1941 when I was ten years old and in the fifth grade. Two years later, the high school added a twelfth grade by moving all the courses up a year from the eighth grade. My mother was sure I wasn't going to benefit from this change. So, in the fall of 1943, off I went to live with my grandparents in Troy, New York.

On the train trip to Troy, I had a four-hour lay-over in New York City. Not being the kind to sit quietly in Grand Central Station, I asked how far it was to Broadway, hoping to catch a two-hour afternoon show. To my delight, it took me fifteen minutes to reach a theater which was featuring Peggy Lee – a favorite singer. After a quick lunch at a Horn and Hardett Automat, I relaxed in a comfortable seat and enjoyed some of my favorite songs. Returning to Grand Central Station, I boarded the late afternoon for Troy, happily remembering the afternoon.

I attended Emma Willard School for Girls – the same school from which my mother had graduated in 1925. There I also learned to ride a horse. Because of my 5' 7" frame, I was given a huge white stallion for my lessons! My long legs had no trouble holding on when galloping around the practice ring. I did feel a little conscious of the fact that I was towering over the other five classmates! Learning to ice-skate was another skill I mastered. I was a miserable failure at my attempts to roller skate, but ice skating was a joy with the wind whistling behind me and my warm scarf flowing behind!

Grandma Kellogg wanted me to learn other skills while in Troy. So she contacted Professor Van Arnam's School of Dance, which gave lessons in ballroom dancing once a week. Being several inches taller than the boys my age, I was lucky to be paired with a tall, dark curly-haired Italian boy. I had no trouble dancing, but my size nine shoes bumped into his size elevens once in a while.

The seventh grade was scheduled to present a play at the end of the year. I happily took the part of a silent Virgin Mary. But the hard part was wearing a very heavy white robe, and standing in one position during most of the play. Gail, one of my classmates, explained that I was given that part, so my southern accent wouldn't ruin the play. On the first part of the train ride home – between Troy and New York City, a fellow passenger asked me if I lived in Troy, New York. How could she tell? I evidently had exchanged my slow drawl for the northern accent that was unique to Troy. My father had come to New York City to accompany me from New York City to Hartsville. He was concerned about the fact that, at age thirteen, I was fully developed and could pass for much older. The coach in which we rode was completely filled with G.I.s, so I was very thankful that he was with me. They were returning home from Europe for the last time.

Eleanor at 10, thinking about the future

# CHAPTER 4

My ninth through the beginning of my twelfth grades formed a collage of activities. During the school day, classes, special events, and other responsibilities filled the day. My year at Emma Willard had instilled excellent study habits, so I was able to feel comfortable with the academic work load. I played the flute in the high school marching band. When the fall football season was in full swing, our band would march through downtown Hartsville the Friday afternoon before the game if it was being played at home. One hazard in playing the flute was the corner swings which, unless I watched my distance from the telephone poles, would put the end of my flute in contact with the black, tarred poles!

During my two years of Latin with my favorite teacher, I was president of the Latin Club my junior year. I found Latin to be an excellent choice for beginning my foreign language requirements, making French and Spanish much easier. To this day, the Latin I see, read, and hear in *Panis Angelicus* is a joy. Miss Baker, my Latin teacher, was the Dean of Women in our high school. This position brought her other duties such as picking the girl to attend South Carolina's first Girls' State. I was deeply honored to be the student chosen. Several days were spent in Columbia, our capital, where girls from all over South Carolina met to learn how our state government worked.

My roommate at Girls' State was Mary, from Rock Hill, South Carolina. As part of our activities during this time, we experienced the actual election of a governor and a Speaker of the House. Mary and I both decided to run for governor – complete with campaign speeches! She won the governorship. So I quickly campaigned for the Speaker of the House and won this position easily. Upon hearing this when I returned to school, my friends laughingly said, "They got to know one of your assets in a hurry!" This was a real high point of my high school days.

I was a member of the newspaper staff for three years, on the student council for these same years, a member of the Teen-Age Book Club, and a member of Sigma Rho – an honor society in the ninth grade. My love of singing was apparent as a member of the glee club and my acting skills came to the front as one of three characters in the junior play – Brother Goose. In my junior year, I also took on the responsibility of helping to plan the big social event of the year – the junior-senior dance which was held one week after the junior play. I was running in all directions. Reeves and Roy McCall were twins in my class. Being good friends, they always took time to try to slow me down a little! I could not believe it when I saw them at our high school reunion, sixty years later. They had not aged like the rest of us!

I had two special friends, Adele and Lynn, with whom I would spend the night to discuss which boy was special in our lives at the moment. During my sophomore year, I happened to be dating a curly-headed blonde football player from a neighboring town. In addition, I was dating a classmate and another boy from several miles west of Hartsville. It took some juggling of times and dates to keep these friendships organized! On Valentine's Day of that year would you believe all three of them showed up at the same time – complete with red heart-shaped boxes of candy? That was the last I heard from two of these suitors. Our family was a member of the Hartsville Country Club. This was the scene of many informal dances, swimming contests, and family reunions.

My older sister, Cornelia, and I even shared the same boy friend, who happened to go to our church and lived two blocks away. Jim was my sister's date several times, and then he would call for me. My father's confusion showed when he would answer the door and have to ask which of his daughters Jim had come for!

Six weeks after my senior year started in the fall of 1948, my family moved to Camden, SC. I bid a sad farewell to my fellow classmates and the high school which had been such a big part of my life during the past four years.

Continuing my senior year at Camden High School was a completely different experience. In the beginning, I felt very alone during the school day. The classes, however, were smaller, and soon, I had made friends with several girls and boys that made me feel welcome. My musical talents found a spot in the concert band. By the end of the school year I had been elevated to the position of assistant band director.

Camden is a very old, historical town, having been the scene of a battle during the Civil War. Our one-story house, with white clapboard siding and dark green narrow shutters, was entirely different from our Hartsville house which had been designed for our family. My younger sister, Ricie, and I shared a bedroom off a dark, winding hallway which descended several steps to a larger bedroom, complete with a bathroom and double doors leading to the back yard. Because my older sister, Cornelia was away at college by now, my brother enjoyed the privacy of this bedroom.

When the day of graduation arrived in June of 1949, I walked across the stage in my cap and gown, shook the hand of the principal, and accepted his congratulations, but my thoughts and my heart were forty miles to the north in Hartsville.

During this year, my father had kept me busy with a creative job. There was a small building in the back yard that was meant to be a stable. His idea was to convert this into a useable bedroom, living area with small kitchen, and a bath. With the installation of several windows and necessary plumbing for the kitchen and bath, his idea became a reality. My part was to paint the outside, put wallpaper on the inside rooms, and refinish the floor. Having already scraped and painted the outside of our house in the fall, I felt ready to tackle this job. I was allowed to pick the pattern for the wallpaper and the colors used for the paint. As my father and I viewed the finished job, he announced that my pay would be $50.00 a month during the time I was in college. This was a real gift, as I would not have to work on campus for my spending money!

The University of North Carolina at Greensboro was my choice for college because of the excellent music instruction. Upon registering for a degree in instrumental music education, I discovered the music department already had enough flutes. Bassoon was my alternative. After ten years of flute, I calmly accepted this challenge, and had a wonderful time playing in the Greensboro Symphony during the school year and the Columbia and Charleston Symphonies during the summer break.

# CHAPTER 5

As I look back, my not being able to return to college for my sophomore year was providential. It led to a future I had not planned, nor dreamed of. But at the time my father told me this earlier in the summer, I was devastated!

I worked for my father during the fall of 1950, but I was anxious to be with college-age friends. My father was now able to pay for my return to college. Since I could not reenter my music major program in Greensboro at midyear, I applied to the University of South Carolina in Columbia thirty miles away. I roomed with a high school friend from Camden and enjoyed taking several courses I had not had in Greensboro. Before this semester started, my church offered me the opportunity to attend the Fourth Quadrennial Youth Convention in Auburn, Alabama during the week between Christmas and New Year's Day.

I happily packed my bag and boarded the bus at Columbia for the conference in Auburn. College young people from around the state came for this meeting. Since I had no friend from Camden with me, I made friends with several girls on the bus. Also, I noticed a tall, dark-haired, very attractive boy among the group. We arrived in Auburn about dark, were sent to our dorm rooms at Auburn University, and freshened up for supper. As I looked out the window of the room, I noticed the same boy I had seen on the bus. Impulsively, I leaned out the window and introduced myself.

We met several times during the conference after that night but my memory fails as to details of our conversations! Warm feelings began as we talked during the bus ride back to Columbia from Auburn. David and I exchanged family backgrounds: He had two sisters, one seven years older and one two years younger, and one brother three years older. His father owned an appliance store in Walterboro, and his mother made the best gravy in the world!

I told David of my family, three sisters and one brother, of my father who was an inventor, and the owner of a metal manufacturing company where his inventions were built for textile mills in South Carolina. Growing up in the mountains of North Carolina, we had slowly moved toward the center of South Carolina. We discovered we had had one similar experience. We had both been selected by our high schools to represent them at the first Boys' State and Girls' State.

I returned home and began my studies at the University of South Carolina. Three weeks later, I received a telegram from David Moylan. "Would you come the next weekend to Davidson so we could become better acquainted?" read the telegram. My heart jumped into my throat! Would I! After conferring with my parents in Camden, I happily boarded the five o'clock bus in Columbia going north to Charlotte. David was there at the bus station to meet me and to drive me the twenty miles to his college.

Weekend visitors were housed in empty dormitory rooms. After getting settled, I drove with David to the Phi Gamma

Delta fraternity house where I met his fraternity brothers during supper.

This was the beginning of a weekly occurrence - catching the Friday bus from Columbia and returning on Sunday afternoon - until summer vacation in May. On one weekend in early March, David asked me if I would go with him to Abingdon, Virginia, to visit his sister and her family. He had borrowed his sister, Jean's, Packard before Christmas and needed to return it. She was married to Fred, a delightful man who was finishing his college work on the G.I. Bill at Emory and Henry in Abingdon - having served in the Air Force for several years. I spent a delightful weekend with them, getting to know this part of David's family. They graciously let David borrow an Anglia, England's version of a Ford, for our return to Davidson. But we did not count on heavy ice and snow on the narrow mountain road on our return. I can still feel the sliding of the car - a very small car!

David was seriously considering attending seminary, and hoping our relationship would last, I made plans to enter the Assembly's Training  School in Richmond, Virginia.  Union Theological Seminary was across the street.

David came to Greensboro on occasions and I went to Davidson for special weekends.  At the last dance weekend of the school year, David made our relationship permanent by "pinning" me with his Phi Gamma Delta pin!  This is still in my jewelry box.

At the end of the summer following his junior year and my sophomore year, I went for a visit to meet the rest of David's family in Walterboro, South Carolina.  There I began to feel at home with his family and the low-country culture.  He and his family had lived in Walterboro since he was in the third grade. My earlier years had started in the mountains, so I had only one experience of seeing the ocean and none in the art of eating seafood!  David's father took me aside after a meal and fixed roasted oysters which he delighted in watching me consume, saying," You will have to like seafood to be a part of this family!" This I did and shrimp, lobster, fish, and scallops are still high on my list with roasted oysters not far behind!

# CHAPTER 6

On one weekend in April of 1953, David drove to Richmond and presented me with his grandmother's solitaire diamond engagement ring. It was a perfect fit - which I took as a "good sign!" We made plans to be married in August before returning to Richmond together for his first year at seminary and my last year "across the street!"

Because of my mother's need to be in the mountains during the summer, our August 20th wedding was held in the Rumple Memorial Presbyterian Church of Blowing Rock, North Carolina. This church had been built of beautiful light gray mountain stone which contained mica chips. Inside the church, the walls, made from this same stone, reflected the candle light we had placed at the front of the sanctuary. Thanks to the cool mountain air, I felt comfortable in the heavy satin dress during the high noon wedding.

A reception luncheon was held at a nearby motel's dining room which all of the wedding party and our families enjoyed. The night before the wedding, my youngest sister, Anna Belle, remembers that I was crying because of my big feet which had been passed on to me by my mother. This never became a problem.

David's brother, Jack, let us use his car to drive to Roanoke, Virginia, for the weekend where David's family was vacationing with his sister Jean and her family. So Jack had placed his car in front of the motel for our departure. My younger brother, E.K., was not going to let me get away without some prank. Not knowing this, he bolted a very heavy chain to our car to make the customary noise of a couple's leaving for their honeymoon. I heard later that he spent two hours filing the chain – grinding his teeth and sweating all the time!

On our return to Richmond after a week's honeymoon at my family's cabin in North Carolina, we rented a large bedroom from a retired missionary doctor and his wife near the two campuses. Taking our meals at the seminary gave me time to concentrate on my last year and a chance to get to know couples in David's class. I taught David to play tennis, which was my favorite sport, and we agreed that we got more exercise, in less time, with this sport than with any other.

After I graduated, we moved to the third floor of a Georgian style red brick house three blocks from the seminary. The owner made us feel like a part of his family during the remaining three years we were in Richmond.

I accepted a fourth grade teaching position in a neighborhood school. The similar academic schedule was appealing and with my degree in Religious Education, the school had no trouble with my credentials. Nancy, the wife of one of David's classmates, was also on the faculty. She had graduated from the University of North Carolina at Greensboro, the same college in which I had spent my first two years. The college had hunter green class jackets with a handsome emblem on an upper pocket. This proved to be confusing to our fellow teachers when walking down the halls during the day, because

Nancy and I were the same height, build, and had the same color hair. One teacher laughingly commented, "I just passed you at the other end of the hall." Little did I know that this teaching job was to be the first of many as I sandwiched time in the classroom between duties as a minister's wife and the mother of three daughters!

David had wanted to go to New York City during this year to meet with Dr. George Buttrick, a minister at the Madison Avenue Presbyterian Church. David gained many insights from this outstanding minister who was well-known for the scholar's mind, the pastor's heart, and the preacher's passion. These insights he carried throughout his ministry. David's sister, Jean, and her husband, Fred, offered to drive us from their home in Alexandria, Virginia, in their comfortable Packard. We accepted the offer gladly since the Anglia was still our only transportation. We arrived in New York City on the day of David's appointment with Dr. Buttrick.

While Fred and David went to the church, Jean took me shopping at Best and Company, a very fashionable department store. Jean outfitted me with the most beautiful dark brown and yellow check wool suit and matching hat. As if that wasn't enough, she insisted on buying me a matching yellow cashmere sweater, dark brown lizard skin shoes, and matching purse to complete the outfit. Her generosity overwhelmed me. This outfit was the favorite of my winter wardrobe for many years.

I had worn shoes from Best and Company before, when I was eight. My mother had failed to find good-fitting shoes for my growing feet in Canton or Asheville. Her next place to look was in the catalog from Best and Company. Being from New York, she knew of the excellent quality. Seeing my downcast eyes when the postman delivered the large brown oxfords, she reassured me that I had a firm foundation!

The three years required for the Bachelor of Divinity degree went by quickly.

Wanting to specialize his seminary training in the field of Pastoral Care, David and I stayed a fourth year in Richmond. Several of my life-long friendships began in Richmond. Martha, Peggy, and Ann were classmates, who later married seminary classmates of David's. Betty and Dan reappeared several years later as sailing friends. Nancy, who taught history in the same Richmond elementary school, now lives in Montreat, the Presbyterian Church's Conference Center near Asheville.

While living in Rowland for the second time, Billie and her husband, another seminary couple, would invite us to come south about one hour's drive. Here David and Lane would hunt while Billie and I compared notes on child-raising and other topics. After Lane's death, Billie moved to Atlanta, and became my tennis partner for over ten years.

During David's second year at seminary, his sister, Sara, came to live with us. She had gotten a teaching job with the kindergarten at one of the downtown churches. Rita, the wife of another seminary classmate, was working in the same part of Richmond. So she volunteered to provide transportation for Sara. This was a wonderful help, as Sara did not feel comfortable using public transportation. Every week-day morning, Rita's car horn would send Sara running down the two flights of stairs and out the door! Fifty years later I continue to contact these friends.

Starting a family was also in the plan. I resigned my teaching position and concentrated on helping David finish the work for his Master's Degree during this year.

Sara Michael was born on March 31st, 1957. Weighing in at almost eight pounds, the darker birth hair was later replaced with a crown of sandy blonde. This topped a round dimpled face with Carolina blue eyes and a cherub mouth. Her first name was for David's younger sister, Sara. The Michael was a name both of us liked – wanting the boy's spelling. At the hospital, the birth certificate arrived with Michelle, but was quickly corrected! And the Michael was shortened to Mike until she felt too old to have a boy's name.

Being my first child, I depended heavily on the current advice of the then famous Dr. Spock. Each day's progress was checked with the open book on my bedside table. Six weeks later found us putting all our belongings in a U-Haul truck and heading south to Rowland, North Carolina, where David had accepted a call to be the minister at the historic Ashpole Presbyterian Church.

# CHAPTER 7

Ashpole Presbyterian Church was a small country church of two hundred members which was built before the Civil War. It is one of the oldest landmarks in Robeson County and is on the National Register of Historic Places. With white board siding and dark green shutters on the windows and hexagonal steeple, this is among the finest of Greek Revival Presbyterian Churches. Through the years, the members have played an important part in the establishment of eleven other churches in the area, giving it the nickname "Mother of Eleven Churches."

Our manse, as the Presbyterians call the house for the minister and his family, was a wonderful white board siding house with porches on two sides beside a big yard. This yard was shared by the church. The high ceilings kept us cool during the long, humid summers. The church had paid for us to move all the furniture we needed from my grandparents' house in Troy, New York. This included their dining room table which had been used for the occasion when Norman Vincent Peale had come for lunch after speaking at the Troy Presbyterian Church!

A significant number of Scots had settled in this small farming community. As the new minister's wife, I was anxious to remember last names. David laughingly suggested that I try Mac or Bracey. I would be correct in most cases.

When David met with the Session for the first time, he wondered how he could find out if our wanting to play bridge in the community would be a problem. He finally decided to take the bull by the horns and ask! Mack and another session member looked at each other, smiling slightly, and answered, "Preacher, we would gladly welcome your wife and you at any of our bridge games." David smiled with relief and thanked them. We did enjoy many bridge games during the time we were there.

I was fortunate enough to find wonderful help in the form of Nellie, a large African-American maid, whose big smile greeted us every week day at 7:30 in the morning. Being an excellent cleaner and housekeeper, she was able to free my time to do other things. Many members of the congregation were successful farmers with families we enjoyed. My roll as preacher's wife was limited to bringing up a very active and engaging daughter. I even suggested starting a church nursery, because Sara Michael, or Mike as she became known, would burp loudly during the quiet pause after David's prayer in the morning service.

The two hundred members included several families who were our age. Lib, Ophelia, Betty, Doris, Lillian, and Florine all had children near Mike's age. Soon we became friends on a first name basis, so I didn't have to worry about the last names! Lillian and her husband, Herman, had adopted a boy, Jim, who was a year older. They would invite us to stay with them on return visits after we left Rowland. Many years later, after Herman's death, I still exchange birthday and Christmas cards with Lillian and Jim.

Several of the members lived on outlying farms within one or two miles of the church. Often, on their way to town, one or another would stop by the manse and leave fresh corn, tomatoes, cabbage, or whatever happened to be in season. This was a southern hospitality we had not encountered before.

An elderly couple, who belonged to the church, lived in a very small, white, one- story house on the other side of the church. Granny Mac and Mr. Johnny, as we came to call them, were wonderful "day-care" help. Often, Granny Mac would let Mike sleep at her house to give me free time for shopping or visiting other church members.

On one weekend in August, the youth group wanted David and me to chaperone their trip to Murrells Inlet, fifteen miles south of Myrtle Beach. Dan's family had a large summer house there which would hold the group of eight high school boys and girls. After making arrangements for someone to keep Mike, we drove to the Inlet in several cars. They had made all the plans for meals and entertainment while we were there.

On Saturday afternoon, Doug and Bobby got out the motor boat and decided to go water skiing. When they invited David and me to join them, David declined, but not wanting to miss an opportunity, I accepted the invitation. They were particularly delighted when they learned I did not know how. We approached the dock, and after watching two of the boys ski, they decided it was my turn. The water was warm as I waded out with my skis on and picked up the line behind the motor boat. I could not seem to stand, as I had seen the boys do, and I kept yelling to Doug, who was driving the boat, to slow down. The splashing water kept getting in my mouth and choking me. The group by the side of the river was cheering me on. Finally, Doug yelled back to me, "Miss El, if you would keep your mouth shut, you would not choke!" Feeling water logged, I motioned that I wanted to return to the dock.

Many years later, on a visit to Rowland, Doug and I were still laughing at my attempt to learn to ski.

I was particularly interested in having Mike go without shoes, having learned from Dr. Spock that this was a good way to strengthen an infant's feet. The soft dirt and grassy yard were good for her to run around on. Inside, bedroom slippers were the only shoes she wore. In early October, as I was holding Mike in my arms after church, one of the ladies motioned to me. "Our circle would like to give you some money to buy Mike some shoes before cold weather gets here," she explained tentatively. I hope the embarrassment I felt did not register when I thanked her kindly and told her we were waiting for the first cold day! David and I decided at lunch that we did not want our daughter's bare feet to cause concern. The next week my first errand was buying her "outdoor" shoes.

Our Presbyterian Church's Conference Center is located in the Blue Ridge Mountains near Black Mountain, North Carolina. In the summer, after our first year in Rowland, David and I decided to purchase a summer cottage there – a needed escape from the stifling low country heat of eastern North Carolina in Rowland. We found a two-story, weathered gray board-and-batten cottage perched on the densely wooded mountainside of Montreat. It had an open porch on two sides and a breath-taking eleven mile view down the valley. The only handicap was the sixty-seven stone steps leading vertically from the road to the porch!

Upon returning to Rowland, David approached the bank with a proposal for a loan to cover the cost. The small town bank readily agreed to the loan. We would spend a week in the spring getting the cottage ready to rent for the conference season. During this time, we enrolled the girls in the conference center's club program. Here they learned to swim, roller skate, and several other skills which they carried with them throughout the years. In the fall, we would return to drain the toilets and winterize the cottage.

The ten years we owned this cottage provided many cool days-readily apparent by the flapping curtains from the blowing wind. Here we also renewed friendships from earlier seminary days. This wise investment provided the down payment for our first home in Atlanta.

David's seminary time had included a master's degree in Pastoral Counseling. So at the end of two and a half years, he took the opportunity to spend six months as a chaplain at the state's mental hospital in Columbia, South Carolina. He had previously spent his summer internship at this same institution. During this time, Mike and I lived with my parents thirty miles away in Camden. David would come over on the weekends. He roomed with John from Atlanta and a close friendship continued after we moved to Atlanta in 1966.

We fondly bid the congregation at Ashpole goodbye and moved south to a first floor apartment on the outskirts of Columbia. My parents were thrilled to have their granddaughter so close. During this time, our second daughter, Eleanor Kellogg, or affectionately called Kelli, was born on August 13, 1959. Weighing in at eight pounds and thirteen and a half ounces, her dark hair, ruddy cheeks, and hazel eyes were a contrast to her older sister's blonde hair and blue eyes. Prior to her birth, my father had been tragically killed in his airplane in Lenoir, NC, on April 4th. So Kelli and our third daughter never knew my father.

# CHAPTER 8

When David's internship in Columbia was over, he accepted a call to become the pastor of the Ebenezer Presbyterian Church in Rock Hill, South Carolina. The Ebenezer Community had been settled in 1785. In January of 1808, the first Ebenezer church began as a chapel which had fifty-nine people on the roll. The second building was a log building to hold the expanding congregation. An enlarged dark red brick building, in which David served, was built in 1955. Three other Presbyterian Churches were formed in the town of Rock Hill by groups coming from this congregation.

The small, two-story, dark red brick manse across the street from this church was to be our home for the next four years. A few days after we had moved in, the door bell rang. When I opened the door, Mary, with dark hair and laughing brown eyes, greeted me with a hug. My mind raced back over the years to the week we had spent together as roommates at Girls' State. We talked for a little while, catching up on the events which had taken place in both of our lives. I had long ago forgotten that her home was Rock Hill.

I was fortunate in finding Catherine, who came in from the outskirts of Rock Hill to wash and hang out diapers. When my friends would come by and see Catherine's car in the driveway, they would not stop to visit, knowing that was my time to shop, visit friends, or play a leisurely game of bridge!

One of the families in David's congregation was very special to us. Sam had the distinction of being the only elder he had ever known that loved to go to presbytery meetings – a required event which David dreaded. Sam's Esso Station was known far and wide for having good service given by the tall sandy-haired owner who always had a smile for everyone. On the counter inside the station there was a jar of candy and a jar of yellow pencils imprinted in red with "Sam's Esso Station." Our girls were using those pencils long after we moved away, because Sam would give them a pencil every time he saw them. His wife, Hester, was a quiet counterpart who fed us delicious meals and good advice on any subject.

In his spare time, David took a creative writing course at Winthrop College, a woman's college a few miles from our house. The theme of the course was murder mysteries – a subject dear to David's heart. Alfred Hitchcock Murder Mysteries were among his favorite television shows. During the six-week course, he wrote six mysteries which the instructor felt had a lot of merit. These were filed away in his desk drawer for later use.

David had always had a masterful command of the English language. His sermons reflected this. With his skill for writing, he would make a distinction between sermons which were made for publication and those that were more meaningful when listened to. Often I would not be able to go to church. One Sunday morning when David returned from the church service, I asked him, "Well, was this a listening-to sermon or a sermon for publication today?" He laughing responded that this sermon would be sent to "The Christian Century" – a religious publication which had already published several of his sermons.

Hunting quail and doves in the pastures near the church did afford David some recreation. Church members with the same hobby often took him on Saturday afternoons. I would flinch every time I would hear gun shots. But his big smile when he came in for supper with a bagful of birds erased the memory. On Saturday, February 11th, 1961, we were just finishing lunch when I realized labor pains were beginning to come. Dressed in heavy boots and jacket for the afternoon's hunt, David ran upstairs for my suitcase, called the babysitter to watch Kelli and Mike, and backed the car out of the garage. The hospital was five minutes away and when the maternity ward admitted us, Mary, one of our church members, looked at David's heavy clothes, and advised him to go home to wait for the doctor to call. We were taken by surprise at this turn of events, as the baby was not due for ten days.

Two hours later, David answered the telephone to hear Mary exclaim, "David, you have another beautiful girl!" He was very upset to miss the birth of Jennifer Mathews as well as his hunting date.

Unfortunately, David was a perfectionist. Even with the help of a half-day secretary, the heavy load began to take a toll on his health. So in June of 1963, David heard that Ashpole was looking for another minister. We bid a fond farewell to our Rock Hill friends, and returned to Ashpole where David would have a lighter load.

I found that moving for our four-year-old Kelli was a particularly unhappy experience. As we watched the moving van load the furniture and boxes into the van, she was sure that her toys had not been included. With tears streaming down her rosy cheeks, I walked with her all over the house and the yard after the van had left, trying to convince her that every toy was in the van. I had saved her favorite teddy bear to hold on the trip to Rowland. This she found comforting.

# CHAPTER 9

The members of the Ashpole Presbyterian Church were delighted for us to return to Rowland with three girls! It was wonderful to move into the same house and Nellie was right there to take on the larger family. Our friends we had known before were glad to add Kelli and Jennifer to their birthday lists, when the ages matched.

The choir director and organist decided she could not do a good job of both. Having had a class in conducting during my last year of college in Richmond, I volunteered to be the choir director. On Wednesday nights, I would go over hymns David and I had agreed would be suitable for his sermon's topic. On Saturday nights, when he was putting the finishing touches on his sermon, we would sometimes disagree on what I thought was a suitable hymn - but not very often.

Nellie did her usual thorough job of taking care of the house and laundry. When she asked me for the girls' pajamas one Tuesday morning, I replied, "Nellie, you washed their pajamas yesterday." Her reply was that they needed to be washed every day. "No, they will be worn out too soon, and our budget doesn't allow for new pajamas every month."

I tried to help Mike with her math homework when she was in the second grade. A week later, a curt note from her teacher requested that I not do so. Her explanation was that now they were learning "new" math, which was not done the way I had learned.

One Sunday night after supper, the girls were sliding down the polished oak floor in our back hall. Jennifer was going too fast. She continued sliding into the living room, falling down and hitting the dark wooden foot of our antique sofa. Bright red blood ran down her face. I rushed to stop the bleeding while David called Dr. Pence, our family doctor. When he arrived a few minutes later, he examined her head and put a bandage on it – until we could bring her in to get a few stitches. As he was leaving, he said with a twinkle in his eyes, "Preacher, just because you work on Sunday, doesn't mean that I have to!" We agreed with him as we bid him goodbye.

Dr. Pence came to my rescue again the next year. Kelli, who was five at the time, was still having trouble staying dry at night. I finally took her in to be examined. As we talked after the examination, Dr. Pence folded his hands and very thoughtfully told me, "Mrs. Moylan, the trouble is not with Kelli." I thanked him and we left the office. When Kelli was born, I was desperately disappointed that she had not been a boy. On some very deep level, I thought I should have had a boy, for David's sake. I had had a hard time during the intervening years keeping this disappointment inside, but somehow felt I had managed to keep my relationship with Kelli on a positive note. From that day Kelli and I went to see Dr. Pence, she did not have any more trouble. I have often wondered over the years if it had been a matter of nurture or nature.

Always thankful for my good health, I planned our meals with the same purpose in mind. My mother had taught us that having vegetables and/or fruits of different colors was more balanced. The girls would vie to see who could become a member of "the clean plate" club first at meal times. One day, just for an experiment, I served several dishes that were mostly the same color. As I remember, we had cooked cabbage, beans that were light brown, and sliced chicken. After valiantly trying to eat what was on her plate, Mike looked up and reported, "Mom, this doesn't taste very good." I laughed and told them about my experiment. Years later, Mike thanked me for the "color-coded meals."

The open yard between our house and the church was a wonderful place for the girls and their friends to play. The circular driveway that extended from the street to well beyond the church was sand, so there was no danger when a bicycle slid or a wagon turned over. During a birthday party several friends joined the girls. While I was inside fixing the cake and ice cream, I heard loud shouts from several of the guests. Upon looking out the kitchen window, I saw Steve, the son of Charles, the minister from the Rowland Presbyterian Church, lying on the ground with his bicycle wheel on top of his left leg. Dashing out, I quickly removed the bicycle and told Steve I would call his parents. Big tears started when he tried to move his leg as I dashed inside to call. The outcome of the trip to Dr. Pence's office was a leg broken in two places. This was a sad ending to a happy occasion.

A family friend in David's hometown of Walterboro, South Carolina, had left him a handsome hunting rifle. In Richmond, he had only one chance to go hunting, but when we returned to Rowland the second time, David had already made friends with several hunters who loved to spend one or two afternoons a week hunting quail or dove in neighboring pastures. David had also acquired two excellent bird dogs who would perk up their ears when they saw him emerging from the back porch with gun in hand. Our girls enjoyed a steady diet of quail which the hunters would keep in our freezer – claiming that their wives did not want to touch dead birds!

After one year, I wanted to try my hand at teaching again. Nellie arrived every morning at 7:30 and I drove happily seven miles across the state line to Dillon Elementary School where I taught first grade for one year and sixth grade for one year, two years later. One memory I have from the sixth grade year was the sound of the loud speaker announcing the death of our beloved president, John F. Kennedy.

On rainy afternoons when hunting was out of the question, David pulled the murder mysteries that he had written in Rock Hill from the file drawer and reworked them. After several months, he felt that they were good enough to try having them published. Looking over his shoulder one afternoon, I commented on the name he used for his "pen name." David had taken the first names of our three daughters to create his pen name - J. (for Jennifer) Michael Kelly. Delighted with his choice, I felt very good about his writing and encouraged his efforts.

Ellery Queen Murder Mysteries, Alfred Hitchcock Murder Mysteries and Bizarre were three possibilities he found on the magazine rack of the local drugstore. The best one he sent to Alfred Hitchcock. One was sent to Ellery Queen and three were sent to Bizarre. After an anxious waiting period, the mail arrived with acceptance letters from all three magazines. We were elated. Bizarre explained that they wished to have all three because this would be their final issue as they were going out of business. Three months before we moved south to Atlanta, the state's leading newspaper, *The Charlotte Observer,* called David for an interview about the recently published murder mysteries. Pleased by the recognition, David set up the appointment for the following week. Dressed in his usual afternoon hunting clothes, David gave his interview to the reporter, who insisted on taking a picture of him in front of the church. We were not sure how to react when one of the members of the church showed us the newspaper with David's picture – in his hunting clothes. The headline read, **ROWLAND PASTOR TURNS MYSTERY WRITER.**

I felt much more "myself" as the preacher's wife during this time. When we came the first time, I was trying to follow the lessons I had learned at seminary. There was a class during the last six weeks of David's senior year in which we were told how to "behave" as a preacher's wife. Wanting to be good at whatever I did, I remembered those lessons and must have come across to the congregation as not having much personality of my own. Shortly after David announced that he had made plans to leave Ashpole and move to Atlanta, one of my friends told me that I "had been a lot more fun" the second time we lived there. This made my heart sing.

David had met a friend from Atlanta, Georgia, while in Columbia, South Carolina. John called David in the summer after my teaching at Dillon and asked David to seriously consider coming to Atlanta to enter the chaplaincy program at Grady Hospital. After David's experience in Rock Hill, he felt pastoral care was the right way to go. We sadly said good-bye to Rowland and the happy days at Ashpole for the second time and headed south to Atlanta.

We did return to Rowland in 1996, to celebrate the two hundredth anniversary of Ashpole Presbyterian Church. While we were there, the three girls visited Nellie, their "second mother" during their early years. She was delighted to see the grown-up girls and even with her aging eyesight, she could see that all three were success stories.

Ashpole had provided David, Mike, and me our first real home at the manse. When we returned with our expended family to our first church home, we were glad to be with a congregation from whom many blessings flowed!

# CHAPTER 10

Our youngest daughter, Jennifer, was not ready for kindergarten when Kelli entered first grade in Briarcliff Elementary School, a short bus ride from our apartment near Emory University. Sara Michael entered the third grade. John, who had contacted David about coming to Atlanta, made us feel very welcome. His wife, Helen, showed me the best places to shop and helped me learn my way about this big city.

The two-story apartment building was made of smoke-colored dark red brick. It was surrounded by tall oaks – the roots of which had given up trying to stay underground. I bit my tongue on several occasions when I tripped over one, while chasing a ball for the girls. The thin walls encouraged us to keep our differences to ourselves! But our neighbors who lived in the apartment above us made up for the inconveniences. Betty and Chuck and their two children always had a smile when we saw them.

Our apartment was very small. We had to store some of our pieces, including the piano. After several months, Sara Michael revealed that she just had to have some way of making music during the two years David would be training at Grady Hospital.

Not far from us was a music warehouse which sold all kinds of musical instruments. We took Sara Michael there, and, after careful searching, she decided on a baritone ukulele. She proudly paid for it with money saved from her allowance. With the accompanying instruction book, she soon was happily playing songs she knew. That ukulele stayed in our family for many years – finally ending with grandson, Daniel, who added it to his collection of string instruments.

Shopping at Rich's Department Store on Peachtree Street in downtown Atlanta was a special treat. Having spent the last eight years in two small towns, I wanted the girls to experience the different departments and riding on an escalator. One shopping trip, however, was not a happy occasion. I had only a few purchases to make and, as usual, was trying to fit the time into an already busy day. Holding Sara Michael's hand on one side and Jennifer's hand on the other side, Kelli was double stepping to keep up behind us. As I turned a corner into the ladies' department, I suddenly realized Kelli was not behind us.

I desperately searched several aisles with no results. Within a short time – which seemed much longer – I spotted Kelli's dark hair as she stood at the foot of the escalator. Rushing over to her, I hugged her, profusely apologizing. Calmly Kelli responded, "Mom, I knew if I stayed in one place, I would be easier to find." Wise words for a six year old!

During the Christmas season that year, Rich's had a special treat for children. On the top floor there was a small train that circled the toy department called the Pink Pig. Dressing the girls in holiday colors, we went to ride the train. Standing patiently in the long line of excited children, the train finally came by with empty seats for the girls. My happy smile reflected theirs as they made the short trip. Before leaving the toy department, I bought a large, soft, toy pink pig to remember this occasion.

In later years, David and I felt they should be taken to a nice downtown restaurant for a chance to learn about table settings that used more silverware than we used at home. Our budget did not include eating out with the whole family very often. One Saturday we went to a recommended restaurant that served several courses. During the meal, we showed them the uses for the second fork, extra knives and spoons.

David wanted to invite one of his business associates for dinner one night. I prepared the supper, setting the table with a salad fork, extra spoon for desert and a small individual butter knife, which was placed at the top of each place setting. I had inherited sterling silver from my mother and grandmother which I had used for all of our meals since the girls were born. So the regular fork, knife and spoon were standard. But for this meal, I had extra dishes. During a lull in the conversation, Sara Mike picked up the butter knife at her place and asked, "What is this for?" With a red face, I replied, "To put butter on your bread." Our guest gave me an understanding glance. David and I later concluded that our girls had been given enough lessons in the use of tableware.

The city life was a strain on all of us. David finished his two year internship at Grady and accepted a call to be a chaplain at the Central State Prison in Raleigh, North Carolina. A fraternity brother from Davidson helped us find a lovely two-story brick house in a quiet neighborhood and the family moved in late August of 1967. I happily returned to being a full-time mom and helped the girls adjust to a new school. Frustration was evident when Sara Michael asked her father what to tell her sixth grade teacher when she was asked about David's job. She first answered that he was in prison! Well, she admitted to the teacher that that was where he worked. David picked up on her frustration and said for the benefit of all three daughters, "Whatever my job title is - I will always be a minister!"

Sara Michael was eleven and developed close ties with Catherine, a classmate, who lived in the neighborhood. When I needed Sara Michael at home, I always knew to check at Catherine's house. This year was enhanced for her by new experiences, such as joining a Girl Scout troop and going with Catherine and her family for Easter vacation to the beach. I became a Girl Scout leader when Kelli joined the same troop.

The Raleigh job did not give him the satisfaction he had looked for, and in April of 1968, a call came from one of his supervisors at the Georgia Mental Health Clinic in Atlanta, begging him to come back and be her assistant in working with alcoholics.

Arrangements were made to move into a split-level brick house in Northcrest, a small subdivision in the northeast part of Atlanta. Here the girls happily made new friends. These neighbors were their classmates at Pleasantdale, the neighborhood elementary school, the following fall.

Four happy years were spent in Northcrest. We were very good friends with the family around the corner. Mary, the mother, was diminutive, with thick, dark-brown curly hair and sky-blue eyes above an ever-ready smile. Don, her husband, was away during the week with his business, so Mary and I spent many happy hours exchanging sewing and cooking ideas. They had three boys; Chuck, the oldest, was Sara Michael's age. He and Mike, one of his younger brothers, were either in our house or in the adjoining backyard several times a week.

Don and Mary had been active in dance bands earlier in their marriage. Mary was the vocalist and Don played a very melodious alto saxophone. So when Sara Michael asked for a classical guitar, Don helped her pick out a fine one. This she played until five years later when, unfortunately, it was stolen at an art show. Barbara, a client of David's, had invited Sara Michael to the show. She insisted on replacing the guitar and Sara Michael is playing the same one today at age fifty-one.

Girls, the ages of our three daughters, are often extremely fond of horseback riding. Sara Michael and Jennifer were no exceptions. During the summer of 1971, Sara Michael spent a week at a horse camp with the daughter of one of our friends. David and I went to the closing program. Sitting on bleachers under a warm cloudless sky, we proudly watched her put her horse through its paces, clapping loudly at the conclusion.

Jennifer tried to build a horse in our small backyard. Using a short piece of a fallen log as the body and attaching four one-by-three boards for legs – she unhappily discovered it would not hold her weight!

Kelli continued her Girl Scout program as an Intermediate Scout during this time and Jennifer joined the Brownie Scouts. They both benefited from the many activities these programs offered. Again I volunteered as a leader and helped to arrange ways to complete the requirements for various badges such as cooking and sewing.

Kelli began the two-year period of wearing braces. As well as being uncomfortable, they kept her from playing the clarinet, her instrument of choice in the Pleasantdale band. So she tried the violin, but soon gave that up.

When Jennifer was ten, we discovered during a routine medical checkup that she had type 1 juvenile diabetes. David's mother was a diabetic and on visits to his parents, Bam, our name for his mother, would let the girls watch her give herself injections of insulin. As I drove Jennifer back to our house, Jennifer asked me if she would have to give herself injections like Bam. With tears beginning in my eyes, I answered, "Yes" as we both reached for the Kleenex box on the car seat between us.

Atlanta had an excellent summer camping program run by the Easter Seals organization. Here Jennifer would spend a week with other children her age, where they could talk about how they felt about diabetes and get good advice from counselors. Correct eating patterns were established as well as activities needed to control their blood sugar levels. Fortunately, Jennifer's diabetes was very controlled which meant that she did not experience the very high or very low sugar levels which caused blackouts and other problems. She attended this camp when she was fourteen.

Then she returned for the six weeks of the camp as a counselor during her four years of high school. Here Jennifer worked with children who were deaf, blind, or handicapped with muscular dystrophy. My heart swelled with pride when I visited the camp and watched her strong arms carry a blind girl to the pool for a swim. A good balance between rest, good diet, and exercise was very important for maintaining the sugar level Jennifer needed.

The summer after she worked at the Easter Seals camp, Jennifer had an opportunity to spend the summer working at a YWCA camp on a Sioux Indian reservation in Dupre, South Dakota. During the school year, she would hike with a neighbor to the north Georgia mountains to explore caves and repel off sheer rock cliffs that were covered with ice. This last "adventure" I am happy to say, she did not tell me about until she had returned!

In January of 1972, I decided to enter Georgia State University to get a Masters degree in Reading. I had found in the teaching I had done previously there was a great need to work with students who were falling behind because of the lack of reading skills.  By going the year around, I was able to graduate in August of 1974.

During this time Sara Michael had entered the eighth grade at Henderson High School. David and I were unhappy about the peer pressure she was feeling in this school. Also, Sara Michael, or Mike as she was best known, decided she wanted to drop the "Mike" and be called Sara. So we started looking for a house in Decatur where the girls could feel more relaxed. Jo Anne, a friend in Decatur, called. Excitedly, she told us that the house next door had just been put on the real estate market and she thought it would be perfect for us. David and I went right over, finding the house to be just what we wanted. Two days later, the owner agreed to a very good offer and in March of 1973, we moved to Oldfield Road.

# CHAPTER 11

In the fall of 1971, David announced that Henry Close, a fellow chaplain, had invited us to go sailing off the Florida coast for a week. I was always up for a new experience, within reason, so I agreed to go. Another couple joined us in Miami.

Henry had rented a fifty-two foot ketch, which the six of us boarded about 4:00 in the afternoon. A tour of the sailboat revealed three bedrooms and one bath, and a galley below deck. I was relieved to see the dinghy, in case the sailboat sprang a leak!

At supper that night, Jane, the wife of the couple who had joined us, asked Henry how much sailing experience he had. I almost choked on the food I was eating when he told us the only experience he had was on a large lake northeast of Atlanta! Sensing our apprehension, Henry went to his charts for the trip and figured our exact location. He returned to the group and joyfully announced that we were sailing exactly on course for the trip he had chosen.

We were within sight of the Florida coast the whole week, sailing south for two days to John Pennycamp State Park, which was a seaside park famous for underwater coral. Snorkeling was a new sport I learned on this trip. I loved the effortless floating movements in the crystal clear blue-green water as we moved above the pink, blue, and multicolored coral on the ocean's floor beneath us.

After dark, our group would play bridge, read, or discuss the adventures of the day. On the way back to Miami, the afternoon weather turned windy and rainy. Our three husbands donned rain gear and headed to the deck to tighten the sails and rigging, while Mary, Jane and I happily played Scrabble. About 5:00, the drenched husbands descended into the living area, announcing the wind had blown the dinghy off the boat, and the rope which tied it to the deck had broken! My heart sank, realizing we might need it in case the boat gave us trouble.

When we docked in Miami two days later, we not only had to pay the rental on the sail boat, but pay for the dinghy. This really hurt David, who kept a close watch on our finances.

The other sailing adventure was in 1978, when David and I drove to Hendersonville, North Carolina, to join Betty and Dan. These friends had logged many hours on small sailboats off the east coast. Their plan was to rent an ultra nunsuch - a thirty-foot sailboat - for several days of sailing in the Chesapeake Bay. We happily accepted, remembering the good time we had had in Florida.

It was a beautiful fall day when we drove north to Annapolis, Maryland. There we rented the sailboat, which had two small bedrooms, one bath, and a galley below deck. With only one sail to maneuver, Betty and Dan took turns tacking back and forth across the bay to get the best wind. The feeling of freedom I felt as we sped south was indescribable!

After two days of sailing south, we turned northward along the ocean side of the bay. The small picturesque town of St. Michaels would be our overnight port. Tired of listening to all the other craft on the bay, we had turned off the radio and enjoyed the scenery as we sailed along. Docking about 5:00, we went ashore to buy food at the local grocery store. As Dan was paying for the items we had chosen, the cashier asked if we were prepared for the hurricane which was coming ashore at St. Michaels that evening. "Hurricane?" we chorused in unbelief. "We have a rented thirty-foot sailboat tied in at the dock!" The man quickly called a helper and asked him to accompany us back to the dock, where he found extra rope, helping Dan and David double the lines to the dock.

Hurrying through supper, we packed our overnight bags and hailed a taxi to take us to the only hotel in St. Michaels. In the dark we did not realize the hotel faced the ocean! After checking in, David and I settled in a comfortable room on the main floor, while Betty and Dan went to the second floor to a room on the left side of the building. Nothing could make the room key work. The office relocated them to a room near us. We leaned extra mattresses against the sliding glass doors. The hurricane hit as predicted. Listening to the sound of the wind and rain left us little time for sleeping.

Before going to breakfast in the adjoining building, Betty went to the second floor, wanting to check for any damage done to our building. The left end of the second floor was gone, which included the room they were unable to get in! The eye of the hurricane was directly above us as we hurried to breakfast. Pressure on my ears felt as though it was pulling them inside out. An experience I can still remember. Everyone at the dining room had tales to tell of the harrowing night.

Quickly, we returned to the dock to find our sailboat had weathered the hurricane with no damage. Greatly relieved, we sailed from St. Michaels toward Annapolis. Upon arrival, we returned the boat to the rental company there.

Four grateful people drove south the next morning. Muted fall colors covered the distant mountains in the Shenandoah Valley. These colors became brilliant reds, orange, and tans on the higher Smokies that closed in around us as we returned to Betty's and Dan's home in Hendersonville. Mixed memories of the smooth sailing and an anxious night in St. Michaels filled my mind as David and I returned to Decatur, Georgia.

# CHAPTER 12

The last house David and I bought while the girls were at home was on Oldfield Road in Decatur, Georgia. This house was built about fifty years ago as the honeymoon cottage on one acre at the back edge of a four-acre farm. The daughter of the owner of the farm and her husband started their married life here, so the name "Oldfield" was very appropriate. The original house consisted of four rooms and a bath.

As the couple had children, they added three more bedrooms and two baths, enlarged the original kitchen, and added a den behind the original living room. This was a beautiful dark red brick one-story house. Later owners added a step-down dining room and a double garage.

We filled this wonderful house with three teen-age daughters who loved having their own bedrooms and two baths they did not have to share with us. Sara was a slim 5' 5" with china blue eyes under long, light-brown hair. Her pixie face was complimented by a warm smile. Kelli, on the other hand, was an inch shorter, with her father's dark brown hair which she sometimes wore tightly curled and other times long and straight. Her wide hazel eyes were set above a curved nose and small rosebud mouth. Jennifer was my height, 5' 7". Her dark brown eyes shone when she described the latest find of some injured bird! Her stocky build was well suited for the many sports which her diabetes needed. The long light brown hair was always shining. Having two bathrooms for our daughters' daily showers was a blessing.

Off the long hall on the bedrooms and bathrooms side of the house, there was a large laundry room, which was big enough for a work table that held my sewing machine. One day, I heard the familiar hum of the sewing machine's motor and wondered – knowing I had not taught any of the girls how to use it. I opened the door to find Jennifer busily sewing the edges of brightly colored material. The end product was small stuffed animals for her dog's toys. On another occasion in this same workroom, I watched her hands carefully operate a small conveyor belt up and down. The belt held small toys. "Looks like the inventive genes of my father are reappearing," I thought with a smile.

The large dining room, which displayed three windows in front and back, had a wagon wheel chandelier hanging from the vaulted ceiling. This was the perfect setting for the antique round table with claw and ball feet as well as the Italian Hepplewhite sideboard we had brought from our first house in Rowland, North Carolina. It held many happy memories of family gatherings on special occasions.

In the living room and the den, there were dark red brick fireplaces which were put into use when we had power outages. On Tuesday nights, the family would gather around a card table in the den and play penny poker or monopoly. Our middle daughter, Kelli, called this night FFG night - translated as 'family fun and games' night. Everyone cleared their calendars so no one would be missing for this event.

The large yard was circled by very old elms, oaks, and dogwoods, as well as camellia and azalea bushes which added red, white, and light pink near the house each spring. In the back corner of this lot was a small stable which had never been used for a horse. It was useful for storing all the yard equipment. This stable had several interesting occupants during the years we lived there. Two of them were a pair of brown pigeons which our youngest daughter, Jennifer, decided to breed. I can still close my eyes and see her standing on the kitchen porch, holding corn kernels between her teeth and seeing the pigeons flying by for a meal!

On one occasion the house developed a leak in the sewer pipe going to the street. David surveyed the situation and decided our girls could dig the six-inch deep by three-inch wide ditch in which to put the replacement. I was indignant! "We need to hire a 'ditch witch' for this job." David looked at me and replied without a pause, "We have three ditch witches in our family!" They did an excellent job, but vowed this would be the last in that famous Georgia red clay.

The house was within walking or bicycling distance of Avondale High School, the neighborhood high school, where all three attended until they graduated. Sara was in a drama group after school as well as in the school's chorus. Kelli also sang in the chorus the four years she was there. Jennifer went to Hooper Alexander, the neighborhood's elementary school. Here she was very active as a member of the tennis team, which she continued for one more year at Avondale. Then she was one of two girls on the all boys' soccer team the last three years as well as a member of the cross country running team. This training encouraged her to try running in the annual Fourth of July Peachtree Road Race when she was seventeen.

A nutritionist at the hospital had been very helpful since the time Jennifer had been diagnosed with diabetes. When we told the nutritionist that Jennifer would want to "raid" the refrigerator at night, she suggested we pick one evening meal that she could eat anything she wanted. So Friday night was designated as "pig-out night," and I would consult Jennifer every Friday before I decided on the menu. This solved the problem!

Kelli and Jennifer were developing definite ideas about what subjects to pursue after high school. With Jennifer's love of animals, she picked veterinary science as her choice. Kelli, on the other hand, had wanted biology. She had had a chemistry teacher in the tenth grade who sparked her interest in this field.

Jennifer had decided she wanted to go to the University of Georgia after she graduated. We were happy with this decision, when the other two daughters decided on out-of-state colleges.

I had begun singing at age 12 and continued, on and off, until I married and lived in Decatur. Here, I sang in the choir of the Columbia Presbyterian Church for seven years. I also played flute duets with a neighbor. For my second daughter's wedding, we played a very complicated duet. This was recorded and played at the beginning of the wedding, so I could be the proud mother of the bride in the sanctuary below! At home, I was nicknamed "the hummer." The family usually knew where I was working by the humming sound. I asked one day if they could recognize the tune, but they laughingly replied that I would just hum the same note over and over.

When David and I moved to Decatur, we learned about The Open Door, a homeless shelter near downtown Atlanta. This had been started by Edward and Murphy, friends David had met. The needs of the homeless in downtown Atlanta had always been of interest to me. When Ed or Murphy would call us to say that the issue of capital punishment was being addressed, they wanted to know if we would join them on the steps of the capitol building to help show our opposition to this issue. Feeling strongly about this, we gladly did when our schedules allowed it.

Wonderful neighbors lived on our street as well as the street around the corner. Couples with teenagers were there to join in many activities. The family next door to us had three boys; Scott, Rusty, and Bradley, two of whom were near the same ages as Sara and Jennifer. One family across the street from us had a girl Sara's age and a boy Kelli's age. The mother of this family happened to have been a graduate of the same college I attended in Richmond, Virginia. We discovered one afternoon, when Peggy was looking at a chart showing my family history back to the Mayflower, that her family name was on the chart! "Cousins" we have remained to this day, though we now are many miles apart.

A neighborhood car pool was a blessing to me, as my teaching schedule did not mesh with their school's. Mary Lee and Ann lived around the corner. Jeannie, their mother, was also a faithful car-pool driver. Mary Lee was Jennifer's age and Ann was Kelli's age.

In the spring of her senior year of high school, Jennifer bought a red-headed Amazon parrot. She had raised the two hundred dollars it cost by cutting neighbors' grass. Putting Heim – her name for him- in a cage in her room, we would often hear loud screeches. Unfortunately Heim had been raised with only a macaw to mimic. She tried valiantly to get the parrot to "parrot" her, but to no avail. So the parrot was packed along with her belongings when she entered her freshman year at the University of Georgia in nearby Athens.

About January, the phone rang and a distraught female voice said, "Mrs. Moylan, I am the RA in Jennifer's dorm. Either I go or the parrot goes!" I could just imagine the reactions of her roommate as well as the girls who lived on her hall. So with many tears, Jennifer sold the parrot to a retired minister in the Athens area.

Jennifer had wanted a horse from age eight. She brought up the subject again. David finally said, "Jennifer, my business is here in Decatur. I cannot move to the country now. What you should do is fall in love with a guy at the university whose father has a two-hundred-acre farm. Marry him and I will give you a horse as a wedding present." In April of Jennifer's sophomore year at the university, she called her father and exclaimed," OK, Dad, I have fallen in love with Tommy Bohannon, whose father has a cattle farm twenty miles from Athens." Tommy was a strapping 6' blonde with crystal blue eyes. He lived at home and commuted to school. On occasions Jennifer would visit his family. In later years, Tommy admitted that he fell in love with Jennifer when he saw how good she was at pitching hay into his father's barn.

Jennifer and Tommy were married in early September of their junior year. Wanting a sunrise ceremony, the wedding was held in a side yard of Tommy's parents' farmhouse. Mary, Tommy's mother, was very helpful in making the arrangements for setting up the chairs for the ceremony as well as providing a delicious breakfast under apple trees in another part of the yard. The morning arrived with clouds covering the sun, but the cool freshness of the countryside was welcome. I proudly watched our youngest daughter happily say, "I do," with a song in my heart.

After the ceremony, David told Jennifer we wanted to give her a wedding present. She smiled broadly and replied, "Well, I'll take that horse now!" Picking out a beautiful golden brown and white Paint gelding, she appropriately named him "Paint." Jennifer enjoyed riding her wedding present for many years.

# CHAPTER 13

In the summer of 1972, David and I made plans to travel for the month of July with our three girls. We did not have unlimited funds for this trip, and I really think this was an asset. David was very creative in planning how we would travel. First, we all decided on the places we could go in the time we had. Our love for the outdoors helped us choose camping.

We had recently bought a large comfortable station wagon that would easily pull the Starcraft travel trailer we found at a camping store. This would sleep six people. Having camped on weekends, we were familiar with the equipment needed, such as a propane stove, lanterns, and sleeping bags which would fit on the sturdy foam-rubber mattresses provided with the fold-out beds in the camper. Each member of the family helped plan and pack the needed clothing, recreational gear such as fishing rods, food, and maps. It was a real learning experience to outfit our family for this new adventure!

Our girls were ideal travelers. David, being a night person, would drive the first eight hours beginning about 7:00 p.m. All three of the girls slept after about two hours and we drove to our first camp ground in Arkansas. There, David caught up on

66

his sleep while the girls and I enjoyed swimming and exploring the state park. This routine continued as we drove across Texas until we reached Santa Fe, New Mexico, two days later.

My aunt and uncle lived in Santa Fe, where they offered us a welcome break from camping. Uncle Walter had built a telescope through which we all took turns viewing the expansive night sky found in the southwest. During a sightseeing tour of the city, Auntie Caroline took us to a restaurant for lunch. Here, we tasted typical dishes served in this area. The tacos were served with a layer of lettuce, shredded cheese, meat, and sliced peppers on top. Jennifer, being the quickest to try new dishes, lifted the peppers to her mouth, thinking they were green beans. Aunty Caroline was horrified when Jennifer's large tears rolled down her reddening cheeks! This was a lesson all of us learned quickly.

The next night we stopped at a monastery in Shiprock, northwest of Sante Fe. David had been invited by a former student chaplain from Atlanta to visit him. The small monastery was located in a grove of short, wide-branching trees which made a good spot for our camping trailer. When I asked about the kind of trees, Kent replied, "apricot." To sleep under apricot trees was very special to me! Shiprock was the New Mexico town nearest the famous Four Corners – where four southwestern states meet. This spot marks the heart of the Southwest. Navajo, Hopi, Zuni, and Ute people still carry on traditions begun by their ancestors thousands of years ago.

Our next stop was the Grand Canyon. After studying camping locations, we decided the north rim of the canyon would be ideal. We got the camp site ready. Then we hurried off to the rim where we gasped at the yellow, tan, and orange layers of the canyon walls across the two-hundred-foot drop to the canyon's floor. Sara murmured,"My dream has come true!" Black squirrels with bushy white tails darted between the tall green pines as we continued exploring. After lunch in the trailer, David and I relaxed while the girls went in different directions.

During supper, we suddenly noticed that Jennifer's face was turning red and beginning to swell. She had hiked a trail on her own that afternoon, but we could find no sign of an insect bite. When her arms started to swell, David dashed to the main lodge to seek medical help. Jennifer had type 1 diabetes and we couldn't take any chances. Finding no nurse there, we were directed to the adjoining camp ground where she received Benadryl shots to counteract the swelling. She could hardly see out of her eyes by the time the shots began to take effect. Her sisters refused to let her look in a mirror – the change was so apparent. Treating her with pills during the night, she was out of danger by morning, and we all thanked God for this.

After turning north into Utah, we stopped at two national parks. Zion was my favorite, with high sandstone cliffs on both sides of a narrow rushing river. Here again we experienced the various shades of tan, orange, and brown we had seen in the Grand Canyon. When I stopped by the park's small grocery store, I gasped when I saw the temperature reading of one hundred and ten! The dry heat was new to us; it felt fifteen degrees cooler.

Heading due east, we returned to Georgia within a few days. After cleaning the camper, David found a buyer for the trailer and was pleased to announce that the price he received had paid for our vacation. His older brother, Jack, used to say that David could stretch a dollar farther than anyone he had ever known!

We moved to Oldfield Road in the spring of 1973. That fall, David bought a new white Dodge van that was stripped down with only the front seat and no inside upholstery. His idea was to spend that winter and the next spring redoing the inside in preparation for another summer of western camping. He and I had a good time putting in a second seat and a stereo system, and finishing the interior for this trip. We put a small cot and large cooler in the back. Then we packed all our camping equipment in a second-hand Starcraft camper like the one we had used two years before. We were ready to start by the first of July.

This time we took the northern route and headed for Denver, Colorado, and points west. Just west of Denver, we took a side trip from Glendale, up a narrow dirt road to High Meadows, a camp ground twelve thousand feet high. Our toothbrushes, which had been left on the picnic table, froze in the rinse water over night. The winter's snow was slowly receding on the high alpine meadow, revealing tiny white and pink fragile blossoms.

Jennifer was determined to catch a rainbow trout in the small lake. Lunchtime came and went without her. Finally she dashed to our trailer, holding her ten-inch prize which we broiled for breakfast before leaving the next morning. The price was high, however. The rarified atmosphere's sun had burned Jennifer's face badly. I treated the blisters with Vaseline, gasping at the thickness of her skin that peeled off and imagining scars when it healed. But she shows no sign of this mishap today.

The national parks of Yellowstone and The Grand Tetons were the highlight of this summer's trip. I can still close my eyes and see Old Faithful's spray of water as it reached its height of over one hundred feet, then falling back into the stone base. But the towering peaks of the Tetons back-dropped by the setting sun were my favorite. The girls enjoyed hiking, fishing, and being amazed at the lumbering dark brown buffalo munching grass a few feet from the road.

Our next stop was Theodore Roosevelt's summer lodge. While we were having supper that evening, the television was airing the evening news. President Nixon was speaking from the White House. When he announced that he was resigning from his presidency, I almost choked on the buffalo burger I was eating!

Mount Rushmore, South Dakota, was one place all of us had read about. The day before we arrived, David had been replacing the twenty-five pound block of ice in our cooler and had accidently dropped a corner of it on Sara's little toe. So when we parked to see this historic site, her foot was in no shape to walk on. We brought her postcards from the souvenir shop, but her disappointment was evident.

Being more interested in the scenery and wild life, the "tourist traps" held little interest for David and me, but the wistful stares from our daughters as we passed them signaled otherwise. The whole family had noticed large white-and-black signs advertising The Wall Drugstore for miles after Mount Rushmore. So when we entered Keystone, South Dakota, and saw the sign, 'The home of The Wall Drugstore,' with one voice, the girls said, "Daddy! We want to stop HERE." We laughed and stopped for lunch at one of the most amazing stores I had ever seen. Besides food, there were stuffed coyotes, as well as shelves laden with so many tourist delights that I don't remember seeing them all. Even though it was well-known for the wide advertising, I was astonished to see the same sign posted at the entrance to a canal in Amsterdam, Holland, eight years later.

This was our last stop except for overnights before reaching Georgia. Upon returning to Decatur, David found a buyer for the trailer and the Dodge van. Once again he happily announced that the price he received had paid for our vacation.

In 1976, David and I wanted to celebrate our twenty-fifth wedding anniversary in a special way. Having had several chances to backpack on the Appalachian Trail, we felt ready to "try our wings." So on July 6th, Sara drove us to the Atlanta airport, from where we caught a flight to Grand Rapids, Montana. Our luggage consisted of two backpacks and one duffle bag. In Grand Rapids, we rented a car that would be our transportation for the next thirteen days – through Glacier National Park and the four Canadian national parks. We were prepared for hiking and for pitching our tent at campgrounds along the way.

On the morning of the second day in Glacier National Park, grunting sounds awoke us early. A large brown bear was tearing up the extinguished campfire in the camping spot - about two hundred feet away. Fortunately, we were across a stream and not within direct sight of the bear. By the time he was satisfied with his job, we were far down the trail, but it was too close for comfort!

The Road to the Sun, which is the name of the main highway between Banff and Jasper in the Canadian Rockies, will always live in my memory as the most beautiful place I have ever seen. My head felt as though it was an oscillating fan as I tried to look forward and backward at the high snow-capped mountains. We stopped at Lake Louise for lunch and were directed to hike beside the brilliant blue waters of the lake to a hillside teahouse. When we arrived, we were served homemade sandwiches and soup which had been brought in by donkeys. Our view of the glacier above the lake will be long remembered.

The next night we stayed in a bed and breakfast at Banff. We had seen postcards of the elegant and huge Hotel Banff built by the railroads. But seeing it in person was unbelievable. Watching guests enter the main door, we realized that our camping clothes might not be acceptable. Taking our chances, we walked in around 4:00. Heading for the tea room on a lower level, we found that the guests were dressed more informally. When we were presented with the bill for hot tea and sandwiches, we ignored the line that asked for our room number. Leaving the amount needed plus a tip we quickly left the hotel.

Calgary, Alberta, was our last stop where we watched a rodeo before flying back to Atlanta. So many memories packed in such a short time were fun to share with our families and friends upon our return.

# CHAPTER 14

David and I wanted the girls to experience various places. During the spring break of 1978, we returned to the Isle of Palms, off the coast near Charleston, South Carolina. Reservations were made for a week at the Tennis Club – a very nice gated community. All five of us enjoyed playing tennis – so this seemed like the perfect place for us.

Sara came home from Boone, North Carolina, to drive with us to the beach. Kelli had made friends with Clay at St. Andrews College in Laurinburg, North Carolina. Since he was on his way home to Savannah, Georgia, he brought her to the Tennis Club. The summer before, we had rented a very run-down cottage on the same beach. When Kelli and Clay arrived after we had gotten settled, they entered a lovely, large living room. Here they saw sofas and chairs covered with brightly colored chintz and glass-topped coffee tables. Her wide-eyed enthusiasm made me wonder if she had expected a cottage similar to the one we had had last summer!

During Kelli's last year at St. Andrews, her beau, Clay, introduced her to a close friend, Clifton Carey, who had graduated in the spring of 1976 – the year she started as a freshman. Clif was a graduate student at Eastern Carolina University in Greenville, North Carolina, about two hours away. There was mention of their dating throughout the year, but I knew it was serious when David and I got to know Clif on several family trips.

Camping was a recreation the whole family enjoyed. One weekend, during a summer holiday for Kelli, David and I took her with us to Mt. LeConte, a mountain in western Georgia. She had camped on this same mountain during the previous January – when her college had had a two - week program in winter camping. So she was anxious to see the same campground during the summer - without the snow. After supper the first night, David and I walked over to hear the park ranger's talk. When we returned, we could not believe our eyes. A large brown bear was standing upright by the open trunk of our car – eating our granola bars. With one hand, he was stuffing the bar into his large mouth, chewing as though it were his last meal! As we watched, he would find another granola bar from the box in which I had carefully separated them from the rest of our groceries. This bar was then eaten just as quickly. Loud shouts from us startled the bear and quickly turning, he left the parking lot for a wooded area near the camp sight. Kelli sheepishly admitted that she had not checked the trunk lid, before she had gone to the bath house to wash dishes.

David owned a small building in Decatur which served as his counseling office the last fifteen years of his life. It had formerly been a house so was easily converted. There were three small rooms for offices, a bath, and a larger room opening out onto the carport. On one side of the larger room, there was an efficiency kitchen. Here he could keep a coffee pot going and store foods he needed. Two of the small bedrooms David rented to pastoral counselors who had been in chaplaincy training with David. They would often talk about the days at Grady Hospital when they had time between clients.

74

John was one of the pastoral counselors who rented space in his office building. John's 6' 7" slim build had to duck every time he entered the back door and his office door. John's wife, Patsy, invited me to join her belly dancing class at the YMCA near North Decatur Road for six weeks in the fall of 1972. I had mixed feelings – not being sure I could make the movements, interest in trying a new form of exercise, and having visions of seductive grandeur which David did not think I needed! This "art form" was just beginning to be seen in entertainment places. Patsy's encouragement found me showing up for the class in appropriate clothing for the first lesson. With her tall, slim figure demonstrating, we followed the music as we tried to duplicate her. I am not sure, but I don't think I ever mentioned this experience to the girls. When I told David what I was doing, he didn't show much interest.

At the end of the six weeks, each of us in the class had to do a solo performance. I was not happy when I finished my turn. But being my usually optimistic self, I was not ready for Patsy's assessment of my dancing. Her eyes surrounded by her shoulder length wavy dark hair, were merry when she commented, "Eleanor, I just don't think belly dancing is something you want to keep trying!" I agreed with her in relief, but concluded it was an interesting experience as I left the room.

Bill was another pastoral counselor who rented office space in David's building. He was about 6', slim, with dark wavy hair above a wide pleasant face. His brown eyes were very serious most of the time, but danced when a joke was shared.

Bill was picking up real estate as a sideline, and had just bought one hundred acres of rolling farmland in Banks County. There was a nice mountain lake on the property, and it was easily accessible from the main highway going to Atlanta, only two hours away. Looking for someone to sell part of this, Bill asked David if he would be interested, saying, "You can have first choice if you would like to consider this."

David came home that evening and we discussed the possibility of buying several acres on which we could put a camping trailer. The girls were headed for college, and any month long camping trips such as we had had previously, were not in our future. After looking at the drawing of the acreage, we decided on four acres which included the highest point of the total package. From here we could almost see the foothills of northwest Georgia. The elevation guaranteed a cooling breeze most of the time; water in a spring on the property made it seem like a good choice. Bill and his family were also going to build near the lake. He and his wife, Carol, bought a large house on property near this land many years later after they retired.

Going to several camping stores in Atlanta, we found a self-contained Scotty trailer that would sleep five. A small bathroom, kitchen, and eating area were between the seating area and a double bed. There was a small gas furnace which made it comfortable on cool nights. The Myers, who were friends from Decatur, had three boys – one Sara's age. They had weekend property within walking distance of our land.

We had many happy times here – watching the leaves turn to red, orange, and gold in the fall, and waiting for the first white blossoms of dogwood to peep between the tall dark green pines in the spring. For recreation, there was swimming and fishing in the lake and hiking on the ridge behind the land. On some of the weekends, we would gather at the Myers' cabin for pick-up suppers, games, and good conversation.

Easter weekend one year was the most memorable. David and I had invited the Myers and several other neighbors to come to the top of our hill at sunrise. Just as the sun cleared the horizon, I led the group in singing a favorite hymn, "Morning Has Broken." Then we enjoyed coffee and donuts at our picnic table. But after the girls were in college, the need for a retreat became less of an issue. The property was sold ten years later. I still have memories of the happy times we spent in Banks County.

# CHAPTER 15

In 1980, when the girls had left for their separate colleges, the Oldfield Road house felt very empty. Between my teaching and his counseling, we soon realized that there was little which gave us a compatible feeling, with the exception of a household project or two.

I was not happy with myself – I enjoyed my teaching, but I found myself not being honest with myself nor with David on many issues. Finally, David confronted me one morning and announced in a serious voice, "Our marriage is not working!" Deep down I knew he was right. My optimistic nature had kept me from taking any action. David had a favorite saying about this. "If Eleanor doesn't like it, she doesn't look at it." Over the years, I seemed to become a reflection of other people's ideas and/or feelings, having none of my own.

The girls would question the fact that I would not stand up for myself when their father would berate me for some inconsequential event such as not having the dishes washed, etc. So when David made this announcement, I folded, as usual, asking him what he thought we should do. His idea was that we should separate. He continued in a very definite tone that he wanted to remain in the Oldfield Road house. I swallowed hard and said," Alright, I will be the one to leave." The relief I felt about this decision should have given me some clue to the fact that there was something wrong with me.

I immediately made plans for renting an apartment in the area closer to my school. As we discussed my leaving, David kindly suggested that I start psychotherapy.

When I started with Millie, I did not have a bad concept of myself. I had NO concept of myself and I felt like a puppet on a string. Millie helped me build a good self concept. This was done through visualization. First I saw myself as a gray wisp of smoke rolling along a dirty city street. During the following sessions, the wisp became a small person who gradually grew to a confident sixteen-year- old girl. The relationship I had with my mother was not nurturing. I would argue with her until I got want I wanted, but never felt close to her. During the time I spent in Millie's office, her ample lap was available for me to cry my heart out. David had enough insight to know I needed mothering to be a complete person. My mother was discussed with detached anger. I really wanted to love her, but the feeling never came until twenty-seven years after her death. This was done with more therapy, during which visualization of my mother and I exchanged pleas for forgiveness and declaration of our love.

Only after I had spent several months with Millie did I realize that David had provided the fathering I needed. My relationship with my father was superficial to say the least – we never discussed anything more important than the weather or family plans. I really never asked him how he felt about matters important to a growing girl. Also, I seemed to have no emotions that I could feel. On expressing this regret to the girls years later, they chorused, "Mom, you would always go anywhere or do anything to get what we needed!" Physically, I was there for them, but not emotionally.

Our second daughter, Kelli, was married on the day before Mother's Day in May of 1982. Our long time friend, Bill, who sold us the Banks County property, officiated at her wedding. I had returned to the house on Oldfield Road to get ready for her wedding.

Being a very good business man, David encouraged me to buy a townhouse to avoid renting. This move provided me with a permanent residence which I started occupying the beginning of January, 1983. At this same time, he felt that we should make our separation definite by filing for divorce. Even though my heart was not in this, I agreed. We both knew that it was not a lack of love which drove us apart. In my head and heart I never really felt the divorce. David felt there would be real problems as a counselor. Thankfully, this did not prove to be true.

In the meantime, I had heard of an opportunity to teach overseas. I loved languages and loved to travel so this seemed like a great idea. I flew to New York City the end of January, soon after the move, to interview with the headmaster of the American International School in Quito, Ecuador. I was in the shower when the telephone rang one afternoon in February. With my hair toweled, I heard the headmaster ask me if I could accept the job of Reading Specialist for his school - Cotopaxi. I accepted with great enthusiasm, but suddenly realized that I did not even know what continent contained the country of Ecuador!! Happily, I notified the school in Atlanta where I was teaching, called all the family, and started looking for a renter for the two years I would be in Ecuador.

I had spent eight weeks during the previous summer traveling with a study group in the British Isles and Western Europe, so I had no reluctance about going to Ecuador. Four of the weeks that summer were spent with my college classmate, Sylvia, and her husband, Jack, who had been in David's class at seminary. Their daughter, Ellen, accompanied them. Being the same age as Jennifer, she and I paired up to enjoy many of the sights of Western Europe.

My fondest memory was our hike on the high alpine meadow above the town of Lauderbrunnen, near Interloken, Switzerland. The snow on the peak of the Schilthorn glistened above us. Three more mountains, including the Jungfrau, rose majestically across the valley. The cog railway that climbed vertically up the mountainside made me very anxious as I looked out the narrow window to watch each wheel reaching for the next cog! When we reached the alpine meadow, Ellen strode confidently beside me, with her long blonde hair swinging in the gentle breeze. Her blue eyes mirrored the sky above as we listened to the gentle sound of the brass cow bells and smelled the pristine air. This was my first experience flying overseas, hearing languages I did not understand, and widening my knowledge of life outside of the United States.

Also, during the eight years since I had received my Masters' degree in reading education, I had been fortunate to teach in two elementary schools as well as two high schools. My work with the Chapter I Title schools had given me a lot of satisfaction, plus the experience that I needed. On one occasion, I had used the Georgia driver's manual to teach a sixteen-year-old boy how to improve his reading. One morning, as I was going to my classroom, I heard a loud shout directly behind me. Turning around, I saw Jim, the sixteen-year old, waving his driver's license in the air!

In March, my mother died, losing a six months bout with cancer. Even her burial did not bring up any feelings. In April of that year, David and I were officially divorced. The second week in August, David drove me to the airport to begin my amazing adventure.

# CHAPTER 16

After flying directly south from Miami for about three hours, the Eastern Airlines plane turned east, and I spotted flooded lowlands below. I knew I was about twenty minutes from Quito, so I settled back in anticipation. When we were nearing Quito, diamond-like sparkles appeared, first on my left, and then on my right. My seatmate, smiling at my exclamation, asked if this were my first trip to Quito. As I nodded my head, he explained that I was seeing the snow-capped tips of several volcanoes rising on the eastern side of the valley. In retrospect, this felt like a prophetic introduction to a priceless adventure!

Academia Cotopaxi was the American International School in Quito. It was named after Cotopaxi, the highest active volcano in the world – pointing skyward at 19,470 feet. The school was a modest, two-story, white stucco building with a gymnasium and a soccer field. Located in the north end of Ecuador's capital city and across a major street leading to the downtown, students, faculty, and parents had easy access to the school. One writer jestingly placed the city's location on "the waistband of the world" since it was four miles south of the equator. The population was eight hundred thousand. Quito is located on one of the largest and most beautiful high plains in the northern Andes. On the eastern side of these plains, lies the Avenue of Volcanoes: Chimborazo at 20,700 feet, Quioindana at 16,230 feet, Antisana at 18,810 feet, and Cotopaxi –to name four of the seven snow-capped volcanoes.

New teachers arrived two weeks before classes began in order to find a place to live, and more importantly, time to adjust our lungs where much less oxygen was needed for living at nearly two miles above sea level. The temperature ranged between sixty-five and seventy-two degrees every day of the year, truly living up to Quito's motto – City of Eternal Spring. Extreme thirst and the equatorial sun were issues we dealt with on a daily basis.

Having previously made contact with a teacher from Savannah, Georgia, the two of us chose a comfortable white stucco house, within walking distance of the school. The rent and the services of a maid, who had worked for a previous assistant headmaster were well within our budget. Peggy and her eight- year- old son, O.J., and I moved in immediately, which gave us time to get to know Gladys and her seven-year-old daughter, Gracie. There was a small back yard between our house and a small two-room building, where Gladys and Gracie lived. The yard was alive with color. Deep red roses bloomed on the side wall. The dark moss-green leaves of the avocado tree were hiding similar colored fruit in the back corner. The thought of having avocados in my back yard made my mouth water! On both sides of the narrow kitchen door stretched bright red poinsettias that were three times taller than the ones we had at home.

Gladys spoke very little English, but having worked in a North American's household before, could understand everything we said. It was such a relief to know that she would boil all the water we drank as well as clean the food we ate to avoid the dreaded amoebas – parasites that would lodge in the intestines until strong medicine could kill them. I gave up eating the beautiful strawberries, because they were almost impossible to clean. She did all the cooking, buying of the groceries, housekeeping, and laundry. Gladys even stood in line for hours once a month, to pay the utility bills. The local mail negated mailing the bills – checks did not exist and cash would disappear! This luxury left Peggy and me free to concentrate on our work and personal lives.

The house was a split-level style which contained three bedrooms, two baths, an upstairs sitting area, a small living room with fireplace, and dining area leading down two steps to the kitchen. Beautiful parquet floors in the living and dining area were kept shining with the polishing Gladys gave them every week. These houses had no heat and no air conditioning because the temperature range was so narrow.

The school helped us in every way. We had six weeks of Spanish lessons after school. Although only English was spoken in our classes, the world outside the school was a different matter. In shopping, for example, only Spanish was used. I learned quickly to bargain. From my travels the summer before, I remembered the seller is insulted if you pay his/her first asking price. All the local foods, including restaurant prices were well below prices at home. But anything electrical or imported was much higher.

The students at the school came from all over the world – being the children of diplomats. A few local students attended, whose parents were owners of factories. Every holiday was observed to honor the students' backgrounds. North Americans were called "gringos," and we were happy to observe our main holidays, such as Easter, Christmas, Fourth of July, and Thanksgiving. In addition the school was closed on all of the Ecuadorian historical holidays. This gave the teachers three-day weekends at least once a month!

We were encouraged by the headmaster to travel as much as possible. The Ecuadorian airline flew us to the jungle area, to Guayaquil on the Pacific Coast, to the Galapagos Islands two hours west of Quito, and to neighboring countries. The price was very reasonable, so we made many trips during our two years.

My salary, which was ten thousand dollars less than I was making in Atlanta, was very adequate for the low cost of living. The public transportation was convenient as well as inexpensive, but very different. Rickety buses, jammed with every age, came barreling down the main street in front of the school – about ten minutes apart. On Saturday mornings, we would ride to the city.

The reading lab in which I taught students from grades kindergarten through twelve, was an exact duplicate of my reading lab in Atlanta. All the same materials were there, and I had a local aide to help during the morning. One aide was the Israeli wife of a carpet factory owner. Judy could speak Hebrew to the curly haired second grader from Israel, Spanish to the office worker who delivered supplies, and English to me. I was impressed as well as grateful!

The fall passed quickly. Kathy, a fellow teacher, and I would play tennis almost every Saturday afternoon that I was in town. On Sunday mornings, I would attend the American Episcopal Church which was within walking distance. It was the only English-speaking Protestant church in Quito.

At the end of November, Peggy told me that she and O.J. had decided to move to an apartment. Several weeks before that, Janet, a history teacher, and I had gotten better acquainted over a spaghetti supper. I discovered that we had many similar interests. We each had three daughters, loved to travel, and enjoyed reading. Needing someone to share the house now, I asked Janet if she would be interested. She came over, looked at the house, and decided this would be a great place for her, while she finished the second year of her teaching contract.

Kelli and Clif wrote in early December that they wanted to come visit me during the Christmas holidays. They were interested in going to the Galápagos Islands, located a half-day's flight west of Ecuador. I was delighted, because a secret agenda I had was to visit the Seven Wonders of the World – these islands were on the list of the Seven Wonders of the Natural World. Jennifer also wanted to join us. So while Janet was visiting her family in Connecticut for the holidays, I had plenty of room for my family.

They arrived on Christmas Eve, and enjoyed opening presents in front of the fireplace. We boarded the plane for the Galápagos Islands on December 26th. I had reserved space for the four of us on a small boat that would be able to go close to the two islands we wanted to visit. One young couple from Germany and six others were greeted by Carlos, our guide, when we landed. He took us to the dock where our small boat was waiting. We discovered that our request for an English-speaking guide was not possible. So Clif quickly retrieved his high school Spanish and served as interpreter for the whole seven days!

Every day we would put on our wide-brimmed hats to protect us from the intense equatorial sun. Our boat would leave early, so that we would be first on the island we were exploring that day. Here, we climbed over large light-gray flat rocks to walk beside the red-footed boobies that were toddling between short green shrubs. Then we would walk on the smooth sandy beach which was sparsely populated with giant sea turtles and sea lions – stretching and yawning for our inspection! The sand on the beaches was so red that the incoming water would be pink.

We enjoyed delicious dinners, and to my great delight, fresh lobster for breakfast. Some crew members would dive before dawn to catch these. Jennifer happily accepted the invitation to join them one morning. Carlos was an excellent guide – standing 5' 5" tall, with ebony skin, and twinkling dark brown eyes to match. At night, we were comfortable in the narrow bunk beds below the deck. The sound of the gentle lapping of the water against the anchored boat gave us a restful night. For this we were grateful after the adventurous explorations we had each day. At the end of the week, we bid everyone a fond goodbye – not knowing at that time that Carlos would also be the same guide for other members of my family in February and my sister, her daughter, and a cousin in March, 1985.

The day after we returned from the Galápagos Islands, we took Jennifer to the airport for her return to Atlanta. Then Kelli, Clif, and I packed our bags for several days in the Oriente – Ecuador's jungle. A three-hour bus ride from Quito put us in Tena and on to Mishauli, where we boarded a large canoe on one of the Amazon's tributaries in northeast Ecuador. This canoe rode almost level with the gray swiftly moving Agririco River – a little unsettling to me. About twenty minutes later, we arrived at the island on which the Anaconca was situated. This jungle hotel consisted of several cottages made of bamboo and standing on four- foot sturdy poles. The thatched roofs looked natural in this jungle setting. They surrounded a large lodge built with similar construction. The two bedroom and bath cottages were very comfortable, complete with a monkey which would peep over the open walls of the bedrooms! The next day we hiked for several hours around the island. Every turn had a different plant, flower, and/or butterfly. The varying shades of green added to the cool morning hike. We saw coffee and banana blooms, several large white flowers, which smelled of gardenias, and huge black and colored beetles, which were at the base of some trees. I tried to take pictures of the iridescent winged butterflies, but when they were developed, there were white blanks where the butterflies had been! I learned later that this is common. My favorite bird call was a melodious note that reminded me of a drop of water set to music. That is an odd description, but I have never before nor since, heard this bird's call. The driver of our canoe identified it for me, but I can no longer remember the name. He said it lived very far back in the jungle and was rarely seen.

On our return to Quito two days later, Clif rented a comfortable sedan to make the trip to Otovalo - a market town near Quito. The car was a real treat after the bumpy rides of the bus I had taken before. Here Clif and Kelli bought bright wool sweaters, wall hangings, and other mementos of their trip, including a complete set of leather luggage to take home the next day. The low prices made everything a real bargain.

After graduation, Janet and I had planned a ten day trip to Peru with my friend, Betty, from Asheville and another Cotopaxi teacher. Betty joined us the middle of June and we flew to Lima, the capital of Peru. After several days of exploring the sights and sounds of Lima, we flew to Cuzco, an hour's flight southeast of Lima. Corpus Christi Day was in full swing when we checked into the downtown hotel across the street from the Plaza de Arma. We were served mate de coca as soon as we had registered. This helped to prevent altitude sickness. The hotel had been remodeled in a very Moorish design with thick white stucco walls. Inside the lobby was beautiful stonework to form the base of a waterfall near a fireplace area.

Walking along the sidewalk near the hotel, there were very vocal crowds of every age dressed in bright colors. In celebration of the holiday, there were elaborate processionals complete with bands, school children, and men carrying religious banners. Across the plaza was one of the most elaborate cathedrals I had ever seen anywhere. Inside this cathedral was inlaid gold on almost every upright surface in the front of the sanctuary. In stark contrast to this dazzling sight, there was a dark cedar choir stall which had taken twenty-five years to carve.

We were ready for an early bedtime after the flight from Lima and the events of the holiday. At six-thirty the next morning, we left for the train to Machu Picchu. From the train's windows, we could see waterfalls hurtling into the Urabamba River far below. These descended from the jagged rock edges of snowcapped mountains. The train followed the river in a narrow valley bright with summer bean crops planted in dark, rich soil which lava produces. They surrounded red brick "rancheros" which appeared at regular intervals. In three-and-a-half hours we arrived at the Machu Picchu station. Here we boarded a mini-bus for the twenty minute climb around hairpin curves. Thankfully, we stepped off the bus and onto the flower-laden front steps leading up to the Hotel Machu Picchu. The nine-story tourist hotel was designed so it would not interfere with the landscape's harmony.

After supper that night, Betty and I went out onto the porch adjoining the dining room. The stars felt unbelievably close. She announced, "Now show me the Southern Cross." I searched for some star group which might have been in the shape of a cross, groping for the answer she wanted! Upon confessing my ignorance, Betty hotly exclaimed, "Do you mean that I have come all the way to South America to see this group of stars and you do not know where it is?" It was too dark for her to see my red face and she calmed down. But I secretly vowed I would find out where we could see it upon our return to Quito!

We were dressed and waiting outside the hotel sharply at six-thirty the next morning. Sunrise at Machu Picchu was advertised as being unbelievably beautiful. We were not disappointed. As the sky became brighter, the sunlight first hit the mountain tops in the west before it actually appeared over the top of the tallest eastern jagged peak – bathing every stone surface in gold. The Incas called it "liquid gold." We walked all over the ruins snapping pictures at every turn. A baby llama with dirty white flanks and a wooly white head was standing beside his mother. Betty and I joined Janet and Gerry at breakfast. I was full of thoughts which went back to 1438 when this Stone Age community was alive with Incas struggling to survive, as they pounded corn in the round grinding tables. I could almost hear them singing and dancing, paying tribute to the priests, and entreating the sun to shine on them.

The train which returned us to Cuzco was like a rolling tin can – uncomfortable leather seats with metal treads on the floor. A round light bulb swung from the ceiling. Taking an hour longer to return than we were told, we were met at the station and went to bed soon after we arrived at the hotel. Sleeping late, we had a hurried breakfast. By nine o'clock, our guide had arrived and we were on our way to the Inti Raymi Festival at

Sacsayhuanan. Ten-foot square stones, weighing tons, were surrounding the festival site. These stones were the remains of the largest megalithic fortress in the world. Costumes of every color were worn by the dancers. Their huge headdresses had long plumes which waved to the beat of the pipes and drums.

There were about one hundred thousand people at the festival. Not all were spectators like us who were watching from bleachers built for the festival. The main event of the festival was the killing of a brown llama and sacrificing it to the Inti sun god. Since we never found a guide who spoke English, we did not learn much about the festival, except that the place was a fortress a long time ago. It was considered the meeting place of the "four corners of the world." I found this fascinating!

The day after the festival we went through beautiful cathedrals with more gold inlay than I had even seen in Quito. I shopped for a llama wool blanket and sweaters to take home to David and the girls. When we returned to Lima I had time to buy a beautiful handmade suit made of alpaca wool. During our last night in Lima, we were awakened at midnight by the desk clerk. A message from our guide told us that the last plane from Lima to Ecuador was leaving in one hour. The city had been under martial law for a month and the military was calling the shots, including airline travel. We hurriedly packed and finished part of the night on the plane returning to Quito, having to cancel our trip to Lake Titcaca in Bolivia.

The next day Betty had to return to Asheville. Gladys was there to help her get packed and we all hugged goodbyes as Betty left with mementoes and memories of our Peruvian adventure. The next day, I got my bags packed, gave Gladys money for the six weeks I would be at home, and contacted Linda. She and I left on Wednesday to fly to Atlanta. When we entered the Miami airport, Linda was showing anxiety about the life she was beginning in an English-speaking country.

The customs official gave her no trouble and soon we were boarding the plane for Atlanta.

My condo had been rented for the two years I was to be in Ecuador. Ann, a college classmate, had invited me to spend the summer with her. She was the widow of a seminary classmate of David's and had spent several years in Taiwan doing mission work with her husband. Tragically, Bert had been killed while flying to a mountain outpost in Taiwan. So Ann returned to Atlanta and brought up their three sons in Clarkston, a suburb of Atlanta.

When Linda had first asked me about coming to Atlanta to continue her education, I immediately thought of Ann. Through correspondence, I arranged for Ann to meet us at the airport. She was waiting at the baggage area when we arrived. Linda was warmly welcomed and Ann drove the three of us to her home in Clarkston. David had thoughtfully made arrangements with Ann to bring my car over to her house. Upon investigation, I found that there was a two-year course at DeKalb Technical School. This was a prerequisite for any foreign student who wanted to enter one of the three colleges in Atlanta. Wanting her to become comfortable with living in Atlanta, we decided she would wait until the fall semester to start there.

I was busy checking on the renter of the townhouse. She had written me during the year that she wanted to redo the half-bath on the first floor, so I was anxious to see how this looked. The walls were papered with magazine covers of bright colors which was very different from the monotone tan it had been before. I made sure there were no leaks in the bathrooms or kitchen and collected the rent.

The month of July went by quickly as I took Linda to visit sights of interest. I spent time with Jennifer and Tommy and made token visits to everyone in the Oldfield Road neighborhood. Sara had contracted with a company in Wilmington, North

Carolina, to write manuals for the company. She had found a nice apartment there and seemed to be happy with her job. David was busy with his counseling center and was glad I was having a good summer at Ann's. I investigated several possibilities for a place for Linda to live after I returned to Quito. Being my optimistic self, I felt sure someone would be available, but the time was getting short.

A neighbor near Oldfield Road called me the last of July to ask if I could housesit for him while their family went on vacation. I agreed and Linda was glad to go with me. Two nights before I was to return to Quito for the second year, I still had not found anyone with whom Linda could live. Waking early, I closed my eyes and prayed God would put in my mind someone I had not considered.

The name of a neighbor came to my mind – one with whom I had played the flute. Little did I know that she had been looking for someone to live with her. When I called her that morning, she immediately invited us over. She needed someone who could look after her two young daughters while she was teaching in the neighborhood elementary school. Arrangements were made for her to move in with the Miller family.

The next morning, David drove me to the airport in my car. I took Mother's cello back with me in hopes of finding a cello teacher in Quito. He called the night after I arrived to report that my unreliable car had broken down on the way home and I had forgotten my hanging bag. Both were bad news. My hanging bag arrived on the next plane from Atlanta.

I had not made arrangements for anyone to meet my plane when I returned. As I headed for the baggage area of the airport, a tall sandy-haired man was walking toward me. It was Frank, Janet's friend from her second year. Waving his hand, he motioned for me to join him. Glad to have someone help me with my luggage, I smiled and asked him how he knew I was arriving. He told me that he had checked the passenger list. Driving me to the house where Gladys was waiting for me, I discovered he had already called Gladys to say he was bringing me to the house.

Frank had come from Liverpool, England when he was twenty-five. He had married an Ecuadorian woman and had three daughters who settled in Quito. His wife had died several years earlier.

School started with a full class load and good aides. Frank called several weeks later to ask if I would like to go dancing at the Hotel Quito. I was glad to have some weekend diversion and enjoyed the evening. It was lonesome without Janet, but cello lessons and private Spanish lessons which I had started the previous year were filling up my after-school time. I continued to date Frank throughout the fall.

In late September, several of the male teachers were getting a group together to hike up Pichincha, the fourteen-hundred foot volcano which I admired from my living room window every day. I jumped at the chance to do some hiking here, having hiked most of my life in the North Carolina mountains. Ann, another teacher, and I joined the rest on a bright Saturday afternoon. We drove about ten miles along the eastern side of the city until we reached the parking lot where hikers could leave their cars.

The first part of the hike went through gradually sloping meadows. Then the path narrowed as we climbed more vertically in single file. Nearing twelve thousand feet, I suddenly was unable to breathe. Gary, who was directly behind me, realized what was happening. "Stop for a minute and then try breathing," he called to me. I followed his directions and found I could breathe again normally. He explained that the oxygen was so thin it took longer to get to the lungs. At almost fourteen thousand feet, Ann and I flopped down on a grassy area to rest. The boys went another five hundred feet to the lip of the volcano's crater. Ann and I discovered small daisies on the ground around us. Just the white and yellow heads were visible. Upon further investigation, we discovered the stems were in the ground.  One of the group explained that the wind was so strong at this altitude, the flowers would never survive under normal conditions! This hike was another adventure I will never forget.

The middle of October, I received a telegram from David asking me if I would reconsider our decision to divorce. Through Sara, he had heard of my dating Frank and was afraid I was getting serious. We talked that evening and I found out he had met someone in Atlanta that he was getting to know. There was one trouble with this person. She could not return a tennis ball! He continued that he was not going to go through that again. Mentioning the past we had had together as a family, he wanted me to give this serious thought. The next day, a large bouquet of orange, yellow, and white chrysanthemums were delivered to my lab. My face turned red when I told my aide who had sent the flowers. I was suddenly aware that the warm feelings I had for Frank could also be felt for David!  When I called David to thank him for the flowers, I said I would reconsider.

Sara and I had already made plans for her to spend a month with me in Quito which included the Christmas holidays. By Thanksgiving, David had decided that she would come for the last two weeks in December and he would arrive on January 1st for a week's visit.  Many years after her visit to me, Sara would remember our time together and comment, "Mother, you were so warm." How I wished Millie, my Atlanta therapist, could have heard the song in my heart!

Gladys outdid herself with delicious meals, welcoming the chance to know my eldest daughter. We took trips to surrounding villages and enjoyed the holiday festivities of Quito. On one trip south we passed several volcanoes.  Sara commented, "Mom, this looks just like the picture in my history book." Before we knew it, Sara was boarding the plane to return to Atlanta. I sadly wished her goodbye, as well as 1984.

# CHAPTER 18

Our real reconciliation had begun in October, when David had found out from Sara that I was getting serious about Frank. The divorce had never really felt final to me – another example of "what Eleanor doesn't like, she doesn't look at it."

I was frightened about the upcoming visit. We both were expecting the old, angry feelings to reoccur, but this did not happen. We enjoyed going to places I wanted to show him and just being together every moment. When David returned to Atlanta, I was beginning to feel a little more confident about a reconciliation. David did not want to wait until I came home in June to see me again. So we made plans for his return during the week of my Easter vacation in April.

Frank and I continued dating after David left. I wanted to continue the close relationship I had started with Frank on my return in August, and I gave him no indication of becoming involved with David again. Telephone calls and letters from David lessened my fears. Unfortunately, Frank and I were singing two different songs. He was singing, "Here Comes the Bride" and I was singing, "So Long, It's Been Good to Know You."

At the beginning of March, when Frank heard that David was coming to Quito to spend Easter vacation with me, he realized that I was returning to Atlanta and to David in June. I could not have hurt him more with this deception. I had gotten to know his three daughters and their families, as well as his elderly mother-in-law during this year. Frank and I had gone to their homes for delicious meals and good visits. So there were sad goodbyes when I finished my year.

David and I excitedly made plans for my return to the Oldfield Road house in June. While I had been away, he had bought a German Shepherd puppy which was from champion stock. For many years, David had wanted to breed and raise dogs that were recognized by the American Kennel Club. Madchen, now two years old, had been good company. He was not sure, however, how I would get along with Madchen.

On the ride from the Atlanta airport, David went to great lengths to describe Madchen and his close relationship with her. The beautiful black- and-tan Shepherd met us at the door. David showed me how to approach her, with my hand extended, palm up below her mouth. Her large warm brown eyes looked at me, expectantly. I followed his directions, and we became friends from the beginning. David smiled with relief as he unloaded my suitcases from the car. I soon learned that her name was German for "young lady," and for the rest of her life, she was a loving companion.

As David and I walked around the neighborhood together, we were buffeted by surprised looks from couples who knew of our separation. I hoped that they could see our happiness.

The summer passed quickly, as I spent time visiting Kelli and her family in Maryland, going to Jennifer's and Tommy's farm, and helping Sara get settled in a new job. In the fall, Madchen was bred to Atlanta's top German Shepherd champion show dog. Before we knew it, eleven beautiful puppies were born. It was a full time job getting them to the stage where they could be sold at ten weeks. Part of the training was to get them to walk in a line. This was in preparation for being shown at the American Kennel Club shows. We had no trouble selling the puppies when buyers were told of the champion sire.

My condo had been rented to a fine biracial couple with two young daughters the summer before. When there had been any maintenance trouble, Juana would call me in Quito. I had called Moe, Debbie Miller's husband, who was in construction. He assured me that he would handle any emergencies such as leaking pipes or other problems.

By December, David and I felt we should remarry. Kirk offered to perform the ceremony. He had been with David in chaplaincy training. We met at Kirk's apartment at 7:00 on December 28th. The fire in the fireplace matched the warmth of our feelings, as David and I repeated our marriage vows. All of the girls sent us flowers of congratulations.

1986 brought many changes. Sara had renewed her acquaintance with Chuck, the oldest son of our Northcrest neighbors. They had moved to Pine Bluff, Arkansas, to be near Mary's parents. David and I were not surprised when Sara announced in March that wedding plans had been made for July. In Gaithersburg, Maryland, Kelli and Clif became the proud parents of our first grandchild, Lisa, on July 8th. I flew to Maryland to help them the following two weeks.

Sara reserved the chapel and the fellowship hall of the First Congregational Church of Decatur for July 26th and picked out the flowers we needed. She found a beautiful off-white cotton Mexican wedding dress decorated with delicate cotton lace. The two sleeveless bridesmaid dresses had the same cotton lace across the top. Kelli wore deep rose and Jennifer wore dark purple.

Upon my return from Maryland, I hurriedly got together all the food and decorations needed for the reception following the wedding. Kelli arrived on the 7:30 a.m. plane from Maryland the day of the wedding. Having left breast milk behind for Clif to feed Lisa, she returned to Maryland on the 5:30 flight the same afternoon. That is what I call good parenting!

# CHAPTER 19

David wanted to try out-breeding Madchen with another champion to produce a different line. So we started looking for a smaller house with more acreage. He would need room for other German Shepherd Dogs as well as keeping one or two puppies from the litters. In October, we sold the Oldfield Road house and moved to Ellenwood – fifteen miles southeast of Decatur. The one-story house had weathered cedar shake siding and a gently sloping darker roof. Rising above the roof in front of the house was a gray stone chimney. Inside were three bedrooms and two baths divided by a large family room with an open kitchen area. The sliding glass door at the back opened onto a wide wooden deck, behind which was a deep stand of dark green pines.

The space under the deck was converted into four dog runs by pouring concrete floors and installing chain link fences. We built six-foot chain link fences around the acre of grass to the right of the front of the house. My dream of an outdoor tennis court was traded in for an exercise yard for the running legs of dogs and puppies!

Becoming a member of the Atlanta German Shepherd Dog Club brought opportunities to show David's dogs. These weekend events were held in surrounding towns as well as in Atlanta. Specially trained dog handlers were hired to put the dogs through their paces in the show ring. By now we had three dogs old enough to come close to a win. But a dog had to win three shows to be considered a champion. Many weekends in the fall and spring of the next three years found us meeting our handler at shows in towns within a day's drive. Our favorite handler lived near the Georgia border in northwest Florida. David came within one win of having a champion dog when Les showed the dogs.

After supper one evening, David and I were talking about the many good times we had had together. Suddenly, he turned to me and said, "If anything should happen to me, I want you to think about remarrying. I want your happiness." I agreed that I would, but quickly changed the subject, not wanting to think of that possibility.

Jennifer's doctor urged her to try having children. For all the years of their marriage, Tommy had helped Jennifer by keeping a close watch on the daily routine which would keep her blood sugar levels acceptable. On several occasions when we were visiting them, Jennifer would want to let one injection wait. But Tommy would insist that she keep on track. So when we heard about the doctor's decision, we joined in their elation. Research in juvenile diabetes had improved and he felt she would be successful. On May 28, 1987, David Holt Bohannon arrived. David beamed with pride as we visited Winder to see his namesake. Two years later, Daniel was born. The boys grew quickly, and soon they were coming to Ellenwood to help David cut the grass on his riding lawn mower.

Sara and Chuck had a beautiful girl named Hannah in Pine Bluff, Arkansas, in August of the same year. Chuck found work in Atlanta the next year and we welcomed a granddaughter who came to visit us on a regular basis.  Her Bohannon cousins would join her in our large front yard when David would let them tumble with a recent puppy. With much squealing from them and laughter from parents and grandparents, the afternoons passed too quickly. Joseph Donald Stowe was born on March 31st, 1989, on Sara's thirty-second birthday. As each grandchild attained some new skill, Sara and/or Jennifer would come to share this with us.

On July 30, 1989, Clifton Carey, Junior arrived.  He was the little brother Kelli and Clif had hoped for. Lisa's deep dimples popped out as she smiled over the top of her brother's bassinet. Her deep-set dark eyes under the straight bangs of dark hair were not so happy.  C.J., as he was called, was taking too much of her parents' attention!

When he was old enough to travel, the Carey family flew to Atlanta to visit proud grandparents and waiting cousins. The dogs that were in the kennels below the deck must have wondered when they heard so many running feet above their heads!

Three years later, when cancer tragically was the cause of David's death, the reality that he would not witness their later years was a deep and abiding sorrow for both of us.

I don't think Madchen ever really considered herself a dog. David had trained her to go to the front door and bark when she needed to go outside to the bathroom.  She slept in a large dog crate beside the fireplace.  From here she would watch the grandchildren when they came to visit – knowing she would have our full attention after they went home.  On occasion, we would let her out of her crate when they were there.  They would rub her long silky ears and sit on her back. In the evenings, Madchen would lie between our chairs while we watched television.  Here I would take the curry comb and groom the long hair on her sides and tail.

When we let the puppies run in their exercise yard, Madchen would stand beside them. Occasionally, she would nip one on the neck when the line was broken. At one time, David was complimented on the behavior of our girls. "What is your recipe?" the friend asked. David replied, "I use the same formula that I use with my dogs. I call it 'The Three Cs.' They stand for consistency, calmness, and caring." How often I had wished for the first two of these three.

In January of 1987, I had begun teaching at an elementary school in southwest Atlanta. My reading lab was a busy place as I worked with children on almost every grade level. One fifth grader was taller than I was and slept through most of his hour. Ben was fifteen and had not been promoted because of lack of attendance and/or failing grades. Each week I would search for reading materials that might spark his interest. His apathetic attitude had not changed since the beginning of the school year that August. Even calls to his parents were met with a lack of concern.

Upon investigation, the principal discovered that Ben was not only on drugs, but was hiding them in a drain pipe on school property. Police sirens shattered one quiet Friday afternoon in April. He had not reported to class that day. Several weeks later, a student brought me a newspaper clipping. Ben's picture was centered above the words DRUG LORD SHOT. This was a very sad moment for me as well as the whole school.

# CHAPTER 20

David had smoked a pipe for as long as I had known him. The smell of Sir Walter Raleigh pipe tobacco had a sweet pungent smell that I really liked. One of my daily chores was keeping the ash trays emptied, but that was done as automatically as washing dishes or making the bed. Doctors had done routine lung x-rays for years to be sure the smoking was not affecting them. Several times he had tried to stop, but he rationalized those efforts by saying that he couldn't see giving up something he enjoyed so much. Subconsciously, however, he knew the doctors were right.

Watching the Falcons lose or win on television on fall afternoons was something we both enjoyed. In October of 1989, David and I had just settled down to watch the last game of the season. Suddenly, David jumped up and said, "If the Falcons lose this game, I am going to give up smoking for good." There was a tone of finality in his voice that I had not heard before. When they lost, he knocked the ashes out of his pipe and put the pipe and the tobacco away on a top shelf in the kitchen cabinet. "Now watch me get lung cancer!" he continued. My heart sank, thinking of the chances he might have, after forty-four years of smoking.

Thanksgiving and Christmas came and went and he had stuck to his resolve. The first week in January of 1990, David's doctor at DeKalb General Hospital removed a small lump at the base of his neck. I was with him when he was asked to go immediately to a different part of the hospital for more x-rays. When the oncology doctor called us into his office, my heart sank. "The x-rays show chronic melanoma lung cancer which has spread to your lymph glands," the doctor reported to David.

On the ride back home to Ellenwood, our emotions were too locked to allow any conversation between us – fearing the future. David immediately made an appointment with an oncologist who was known to recommend very aggressive treatments. He started chemotherapy and radiation the next week. These treatments left him feeling very tired in the morning. But his mornings were free because his clients at his counseling center usually came between 4:00 and 8:00 at the end of a work day. Fortunately, his office was only three blocks from DeKalb General Hospital.

My teaching had changed from an Atlanta elementary school to the remedial lab at Dekalb Community College in Clarkston. The students who needed help would come between 2:00 and 6:00 every day. This gave me the mornings at home. Every Friday we would get a report on the blood work for that week. If David's white blood cell count was low, his immune system would not permit visits from the family on the weekend. So we "lived" from Friday to Friday!

Joseph, who was almost two, was very attached to his grandfather. Sitting in David's lap on the riding lawnmower for the weekly grass cutting or in David's easy chair in front of the fireplace brought contented smiles.

By late March, x-rays showed no cancer in his lungs. We were elated! David's doctor let us know that this type of cancer

was chronic and the length of a remission would depend on his treatments. More space was put between the chemotherapy appointments and radiation was reduced to once a month because of the side effects. David was able to keep working until July of 1992.

There were two particularly happy events during this time. In July of 1991, all of David's family gathered at the Isle of Palms to celebrate his 60th birthday. Three condos facing the beach housed his older sister and her family from Roanoke, Virginia, his younger sister and her family, and Sara and her family from Decatur. His brother and his family drove over from nearby Walterboro. Kelli and her children flew to Charleston from Maryland. The weekend was full of swimming, playing tennis, and swapping stories between cousins – ending in a big birthday supper at our condo.

The other event was a two-week vacation in San Jose, the capital of Costa Rica. My Quito housemate, Janet, and her husband, Hugh, had bought a retirement home high above the city. We could see the shining waters of the Pacific Ocean on the other side of this narrow country from their front porch. During this time, we visited the famous cloud forest – catching a very rare sight of the quetzal bird of Guatemala. We also spent one evening at the foot of the famous Arenal volcano. We could actually feel the heat of the dark red fiery lava flow and hear the large volcanic rocks as they rumbled down the side we were facing. The next morning every plant, road, and roof top was covered with fine pink ash as we drove back toward San Jose. With daily rests, David was pleased that his energy level had stayed high during this vacation.

Many weekend afternoons were spent getting acquainted with David's financial picture. I had been keeping his client's accounts on the computer's Quicken program, but I had no knowledge of where he was putting his earnings.

One thing David was adamant about was making sure that I had long term health insurance. Bob and Rita were a couple we had met when we were in seminary together. Bob's wife, Rita, had been the one to drive his sister, Sara, to work, when she lived with us in Richmond. Now Bob worked for the Presbyterian Church, U.S.A.'s Board of Annuities in Atlanta. One of his jobs was to help set up a policy that we were looking for. So Bob came over one afternoon and told us all of the options we had for this insurance. David was so pleased with his expertise, that he had Bob design the whole policy, even to picking out the insurance company he felt would be best. Fortunately, I have never had to use this policy, but I have been very happy over the fact that the premiums have never been increased more than a few dollars in the last seventeen years.

We managed to cover many subjects, but we never discussed how he wanted his funeral. When David was dealing with a funeral director in one of his pastorates, the subject of cost would come up. Shaking his head, he told me that when plans were made for his funeral, he wanted me to ask to see the most expensive casket. Then I was to request that he be buried in the shipping box of that casket! "Money is for the living – not for the dead." His only other request for his funeral was that the beginning of Beethoven's Ninth Symphony be played.

David's cancer returned in full force the end of July in 1992. His treatment was increased but had little effect. He did return to Walterboro the second weekend of August for his forty-third high school reunion. His head had been completely shaved for many months, after reaction to chemotherapy had made his hair fall out. After the reunion dinner, class members reminisced about all the football games David had helped to win, as well as other honors he had brought to their class. He stood briefly to give a response, knowing this would be the last time he would see them. The standing applause brought tears to his eyes as well as mine.

The middle of October, David was taken to the hospital, suddenly unable to stand or walk. The doctor diagnosed blood poisoning, a reaction to his chemotherapy. For three weeks, the nurses and I fed him the little he would eat and tried to keep him comfortable. The last week the cancer had spread to his bones in his left leg and only morphine could ease the pain.

On Tuesday, the 2nd of November, David was dismissed from the hospital. The doctor told us he could not live long and to call the family. Hospice was hired to take care of him at home, and Kelli flew down from Maryland to spend this week with us. Madchen knew her beloved master was sick when he could not tolerate her near him. His family and several close friends came to say goodbye. When the hospice nurse came to check his medications on the following Monday, he had no pulse. Kelli and I had let him rest that morning and did not realize he was not breathing. In immediate shock, I could not think of how to proceed. The nurse called the ambulance, the doctor, and the funeral home we had decided upon. The funeral home in Walterboro drove to Decatur, and took his body for the burial in the family plot there.

Sara and her children drove Kelli and me to Walterboro after supper the next day. Joseph had had a very hard time realizing his grandfather was dead. I looked back from my front seat during the four- hour trip to see Joseph looking intently at the stars in the early evening sky. "I can see Granddaddy smiling at me from heaven," he whispered loudly. We all felt strangely comforted.

The funeral service was held on Wednesday in David's home church. He had worshipped in this church since he was eight years old and was the only member to become a minister. As we drove back to Decatur, I silently asked David to forgive me for not having the courage to ask for the shipping box his casket had come in!

A memorial service was held the next Monday, November 16th, at Columbia Presbyterian Church. Sara found a professional trumpet player who agreed to play at the service. The ending notes of "The Strife Is O'er, The Battle Done" floated over the heads of the two hundred friends and family that had gathered. Betty, the director of the DeKalb General Hospital's Cancer Center gave the eulogy. She spoke of this opportunity we had to celebrate his life, to acknowledge his significant journey to understand, and to appreciate the resilience of the human spirit. One thing she would always remember was David's faith in God – stating that it was intricately woven into the fabric of his life. Various former clients and friends rose to add to her remarks for the rest of the hour. It was a real celebration of a life that had been mine to share for thirty-nine years. "Carpe diem" is still the "password" at the Cancer Center. The English translation is "seize the day." This David had done each day since his diagnosis with his whole heart!

# CHAPTER 21

After David's death, my life felt like it was on emotional autopilot. Betty, my long-time friend, now lived in Arden – a suburb south of the city of Asheville. When she called to invite me to come there for Thanksgiving weekend, I gladly accepted. Betty was working hard as a real estate broker and welcomed the chance to talk over old times.

The girls had already made their plans for the holiday, so I felt free to go. A close friend of Betty's had invited us over for dinner around two o'clock on Thanksgiving Day. The four-hour drive from Ellenwood to Arden was easy and I arrived in time to change clothes before leaving for her friend's house. Several other people were there when we arrived and I was greeted warmly.

After dinner, Betty and I left to return to her house. Making ourselves comfortable, Betty looked me squarely in the eyes and said, "Now that you are alone, what do you plan to do?" Without a moment's hesitation, I replied, "I am moving to Asheville." The long pause made me wonder how she felt about my announcement! It did not take long for her to tell me that she knew just the right house for me. Betty described a small house that was under construction about a five minute's drive from her house. If she could contact the builder, it would be possible to see this house while I was visiting her.

At 3:00 p.m. the next day, Betty and I drove up a narrow road that curved up and around Mount Royal. This was a small community that had been established on a quiet and peaceful foothill for a long time. After leaving the main road, we passed several small one-story houses, before driving down a steep driveway beside a soft yellow wood frame house trimmed in white. The house had been built on a steeply sloping lot which was surrounded by deep woods of tall pines and poplars. After walking up a narrow path leading to the front door, Betty knocked loudly. A slim brunette opened the door immediately. When introductions had been made, I looked across the small living room to sliding glass doors opening onto a narrow deck. Beyond the deck were distant high mountains shining in the afternoon sun. The view made my heart sing!

Built for one person, the arrangement of the bedrooms, living room, dining room, and kitchen looked like what I wanted. Betty and I returned the next morning to discuss the contract which we both felt was very acceptable. I gave her a check for the down payment and promised to return to pick out the colors for the rooms and carpet, tiles for the kitchen and baths, and light fixtures when these decisions needed to be made.

The girls were delighted when I returned to Ellenwood after the weekend and told them I had bought a house in Arden. They could still remember the happy days they had spent in Montreat, the Presbyterian Church's Conference Center near Black Mountain. We had owned a summer cottage there for the ten years of David's pastorates. Memories of my own childhood in nearby Canton and Asheville relieved any doubts about my move.

The reality of David's death was enforced as I dealt with what to do with his things – like the gun which had been so loved. Hunting was out of the question when we moved to Atlanta so many years ago. As I pulled it out of its leather case, I thought of his namesake, David Bohannon. On my next visit to Jennifer and Tommy's farm, I explained that I really wanted their son to have it. They were pleased with my decision, but here again it remained in the corner of a closet waiting for their David to grow up! On one visit many years later, I noticed that Tommy had completely reworked the gun. He had carefully decorated the new, light brown oak stock with a beautiful design. The gray metal part of the new barrel shone from many hours of rubbing. When David was old enough to use the gun, he could hit a deer at three hundred and fifty feet – an accomplishment his grandfather would have been proud of.

On one of my more frequent visits to Sara and Chuck's house in Decatur, I was met at the door by four-year-old Hannah. I could not believe the outfit she had chosen for the day. A flowered blouse fitted over the top of her purple ballerina outfit with blue jean shorts peeping from under the frilly skirt. A floppy hat covered her light brown hair and cowboy boots completed the picture. "Hannah," I exclaimed, "did you get to choose what to wear this morning?" With a wide grin, she danced around me to show all sides! When I voiced my very obvious concern, Sara laughingly replied, "Don't worry, Mom. The theory is that if you let them make their own choices at the age of four, they will make better choices when they are six months older." Exactly six months to the day, Hannah proudly showed me her closet and how her clothes were hung according to color and style.

The last week in January, a chaplain from DeKalb General Hospital led a week's group therapy session for family members of cancer victims. This was sponsored by the Cancer Center of the hospital. Betty, from the Center, strongly urged me to join the group. I noticed that other members of the group could express deep feelings of grief. My responses, however, felt contrived. I shook the chaplain's hand at the conclusion of the last session and left without comment.

During the second week of February, my youngest sister, Anna Belle, invited me to come to visit in Tucson, Arizona. She had bought a small, one-story, white stucco house at the foot of the mountains outside of town. There was a wide, red tile patio facing the mountain.

While she was at work, I would sit for several hours, soaking up the warm Arizona sun. The wide expanse of the bright blue southwestern sky above me was a new experience. I felt a continuing sorrow over the fact that I did not tell David goodbye before he died. A strange closeness to him filled my heart as I continued to look at the sky. So I spoke the words I had wanted to say. Then I felt as though a soft blanket had been wrapped around my shoulders and the grief was lifted from my heart. This feeling remains after almost seventeen years.

It was early March before I found a buyer for the Ellenwood house. Wanting someone who would be a good neighbor to my friends there was important to me. When a young woman who needed a house with a central location for her business as a sales representative saw the size and surrounding yard, she bought it quickly.

On March 1st, I resigned my teaching position at Dekalb Community College and completed all the forms necessary for setting up my retirement benefits I would receive from the State of Georgia's Merit System. All of the other financial decisions had been made the month following David's death. During one of my trips back to Arden to check on details for the new house, I had secured the services of an accountant to handle all the tax issues before April 15th.

Kelli and Clif drove down during the Easter weekend and took several family pieces I would not need in Arden. Sara and Jennifer came to help with the final packing. After saying my goodbyes to my family and friends of so many years, I left Ellenwood on April 6th, driving ahead of the moving van.

As I turned west from Greenville, it was not long before I could see the blue of the  mountains' ridges  - aptly named the Blue Ridge Mountains. Strong emotions began to bubble within me. My lifelong associations with these mountains were part of this, and as the car started to climb, I sang, "I go to the hills where my heart is lonely; I know I will hear songs I've heard before. The hills fill my heart with the sound of music and I'll sing once more." Rodgers' and Hammerstein's words and music were very comforting.

The builder met me at the door when I arrived to give me the keys and go over all the details. Highly polished white oak floors greeted me. White and pink dogwoods were peeking out from between the dark brown trunks of the pine trees near the house. Their heart-shaped blossoms seemed to call out, "Surprise!" The trees on the far distant mountains were now spring's lighter shade of green. Betty had contacted the telephone company. The electricity and water were on.

Before I had left Ellenwood, a former seminary classmate of David's called me to see if I would be interested in joining a group she was taking to Greece at the end of April. The tour would be visiting all of the places that the missionary Paul had visited. Sara also introduced me to Winnie, a recent widow like myself, who was looking for someone to share a double occupancy on the tour. When I discovered that Winnie was a retired librarian and the widow of a Lutheran minister in Atlanta, as well as having children the same age a mine, we did not take long to add our names to the tour group's list. After sixteen years, we are still close friends.

It was not long before I had the house arranged to my satisfaction and learned my way around the small town of Arden. The tax consultant completed my income tax forms and had them ready for me to sign. When I saw the bill, I realized I needed someone who could handle David's investments. Being the "saver" in our marriage, he had invested our income in numerous companies. Betty gave me the name of her financial advisor in Hendersonville – fourteen miles south of Arden. I made an appointment with Peter and was very pleased with his ideas as well as his price. Peter made it very clear from the time we met that he was there to advise me about my investments. "But you will be the one to decide what you want to do with your money," he concluded. Through the years he has not taken any unnecessary risks and has kept an eagle eye on the ups and downs of the market – here and abroad. Thanks to him, I am still able to afford my various needs as well as desires.

Madchen felt at home in the new house very quickly. I enjoyed taking her on walks up the road that led past several simple wooden houses, and I soon got to know the neighbors within walking distance of the house. Sara and Chuck brought the grandchildren to Asheville during June. Before the summer was over, the other two girls and their families had enjoyed the new house and were happy about my move.

I had been a member of the International Reading Association for many years. During April, I received a notice from them, advertising the annual meeting. It was going to be held in Melbourne, Australia for the first time. A tour was offered to its members. This tour included one week in New Zealand before the conference, followed by two weeks in Australia - one week for the conference and one week of sightseeing up the eastern coast as far as Cairns. I did not waste any time talking Betty into going with me. My excitement ran high when I learned about the chance to snorkel at the Great Barrier Reef – considered the best by my brother who had been there. The conference in Melbourne included getting to know the Aboriginal writers and illustrators of children's books. My book shelf still holds children's books I purchased at this conference.

On June 27th, Betty and I joined twenty reading specialists from Maryland at the Los Angeles airport. Boarding Australian Air Lines at about 8:00 that evening, we settled back for the fourteen-hour flight to Auckland, the capital of New Zealand. Only one member of the group was sad when she realized that her birthday was on the day we lost going over the International Date Line.

This bustling port city lies on the eastern side of the narrow North Island. Our tour guide settled us into a nice hotel, explaining that we would see Auckland at the end of our week there. We drove south to Christ Church, a lovely small city with a definite British feel, and our first stop on the South Island. Our warm jackets and sweaters were welcome on their winter days. The next morning we stopped for an hour to observe the reading class of an elementary school – very much the size of our classes at home. The tall young teacher conducted his class with no nonsense which made it feel sterile to me – but the students performed without hesitation. As we continued south to Queensland, the tall jagged Southern Alps were covered with glistening snow.

Before leaving the South Island, we toured the icy blue waters of Milford Sound. Here we pulled our wool scarves tightly around our necks as arctic winds blew between the jagged peaks of the glaciers. Another new experience was watching Australian sheep dogs round up a large flock of sheep on a hillside farm.

On Saturday, we returned to Auckland to spend one day in the capital. We had lunch at a park high above the city. As we lined up along a strong steel fence at the edge of the park, we could see a bowl shape below us that was covered with grass.

Our guide told us that it was the crater of an ancient volcano – one of sixty-one volcanoes in New Zealand. That afternoon we flew to Melbourne to begin the conference.

Thankfully, the conference was held at the hotel where everyone was staying. The small balcony off our room on the fifteenth floor overlooked the narrow river that runs through the city. Here we could watch early morning boats as well as large ships going to and from countries around the world. Before leaving Melbourne, our tour group drove south for the day. At several wildlife parks we could watch the kangaroos hopping here and there. The short fat brown furry wombats were not as friendly. By suppertime, we had reached Phillip Island in the cold waters of Bass Strait. Here we quickly found places on low wooden bleachers which faced the waters of the strait. Just as the sun went below the horizon, the parade of fairy penguins began. The stadium lights above us reflected off the sleek dark blue fur on their thirteen-inch bodies. They slowly waddled in pairs toward their burrows under our seats! Nowhere else in the world can these penguins be found. The week passed quickly and by Monday we were on our way to Sydney.

The two days we spent in Sydney were filled with more visits to wildlife parks, a tour of the world-renowned opera house, and a visit to the best zoo I have ever seen. Here we spent a long time admiring a white leopard with multiple splotchy black spots.

We arrived at Cairns, our last stop of the tour. Betty and I were happy with the small town's one-story native hotel after the high rise in Melbourne. The dining area was located on a wide patio. This led to a small garden area which included a circular pool lined with native stones. Taking a leisurely swim after supper, I was admiring the arrangement of stars in the midnight blue sky. Suddenly, I grabbed Betty's arm and pointed to a small group of four equidistant stars twinkling above us. "There," I shouted. "There is the Southern Cross!" After my failure in Peru, I had made sure I would recognize it. I could almost see her smile in the low lights around the pool.

My big moment of the whole trip came the next morning when our group packed our bathing suits for the boat ride to the Great Barrier Reef. By 10:00, the small boat had dropped anchor within sight of the beach where we were going to snorkel. I was almost dizzy with excitement. Walking slowly into the clear blue water, I began to float above small fish that were gold, silver, blue, and pink swimming above and among the multiple shades of orange, green, and tan coral. These will have to stay in my memory; there was no possibility of taking pictures!

Before leaving this part of Australia, we toured an amazing rainforest and rode in an old narrow gauge train up the mountainside to the best butterfly sanctuary I had ever seen. My friends still admire the T-shirt I bought there with examples of their most unusual butterflies.

I had taken Madchen to a well-maintained kennel for boarding while I was in Australia. It was small and on a low mountain ridge where she could get good exercise. When I went to pick her up, the owner looked relieved when I paid my bill. "Did she behave herself while I was away?" I asked – not expecting a negative reply. As we entered the kennel area, I noticed that she had been separated from the other dogs. The owner told me that when Madchen was fed the first day, she would carefully pick up the edge of her large metal pan and sling her food through the chain link divider with such force that the food would travel through the remaining three kennels! On our return trip to the house from the kennels, Madchen and I had a long talk about her behavior. Her warm, brown eyes did not reflect any remorse as far as I could tell.

In early August, I received a call from Columbia Seminary in Decatur. My friend, Sara, who had led the trip to Greece, wanted to know if I would be interested in joining a small group that was going to Israel, the last of September. The leader, Dr. Dewitz, a retired seminary professor of Biblical Studies, was a former Oldfield Road neighbor whom I knew well. The opportunity to visit all of the places I had read about since I was a child was too good to miss.

The 20th of September, the group flew from Atlanta to Tel Aviv, after changing planes in Frankfort, Germany. Before we landed, Dr. Dewitz gave us the eleventh commandment - "adjust." This advice was really needed during the following ten days! Our guide, Sari, greeted us warmly as we left the baggage area of the airport. With a wide smile, she said, "This is The Holy Land but we are up to our necks with sin." Sari was a Bedouin with a degree in History from the University of Damascus. As we rode by the different points of interest, I felt as if a walking history book was giving us the descriptions!

Caesarea was our first stop. Here was the place where Peter had baptized the first Gentile convert – a centurion named Cornelius. We learned quickly that churches had been built over most of the places recorded in the Bible. At Cana of Galilee, the church marked the place where Jesus had changed the water into wine. Traveling south in this narrow country, we could see to our left the blue clear waters of the Sea of Galilee. I was particularly interested in the trees along the road. Some were date and pomegranate. Eucalyptus had been brought here from Australia to soak up the marshes. Later we saw grapefruit, lemon, and olive trees. We learned that most of the miracles Jesus performed were around the Sea of Galilee.

The third day of our tour took us to the Dead Sea. It is seven hundred feet below sea level and the saline content of the water nears ninety percent. Three of us tried swimming in the arctic blue waters which were very salty and slimy. We bounced up and down like corks, never being able to get our feet under water. There were cold showers available and it took five attempts to get all the slime of the salt water off my skin! The dry heat during our tour was extreme – especially in the Dead Sea area.

On our return to Jerusalem, we stopped by the ancient city of Jericho, where I saw another Tree of Life. This one was on the guest room floor in Hirsham's Palace. The faded blues, reds, and grays of the stone were undeniably fashioned in the shape of the Tree of Life. After Jericho, we stopped by the banks of the Jordan River to see the place where Jesus had been baptized. I was excited to actually put my feet in this river!

We had three days left of the tour when we stopped by Bethlehem for a lunch break. Here was the large, ornate Church of the Nativity on a very narrow city street. We entered the dark entrance to find that we had to descend three narrow sets of stairs to reach the actual spot where Jesus had been born. A large brass star on the floor of a small enclosure marked the spot, and I spent several minutes realizing the significance of this place. After we got to Jerusalem, our pace quickened. One noon we sat on the sloping grass field where the shepherds heard the angels announcing Christ's birth. The day before we left we were resting on narrow, slightly indented, stone steps when our guide told us that Jesus had actually walked on these steps. One of my favorites of the tour was visiting the chapel in which Marc Chagall's stained glass windows depicted several Bible figures in brilliant blues, greens, and reds.

The day before we returned to the United States, we toured the Wailing Wall, Golgatha, and the church which had been built over the place where Jesus and his disciples held their last supper. It was called Saint Peter in Gallicantu which means "at the cock's crow." The local guide explained that here we are also commemorating Peter's denial of Christ in the courtyard of the High Priest, Caiaphas, as well as the apostle's repentance after he had heard the cock crow three times and remembered Jesus' words to him.

As our tour group settled back in our seats on the airline's return to Atlanta, I closed my eyes and remembered many of the amazing sights I had seen. When I later would read the Biblical accounts, I felt truly blessed to actually have been in these places.

# CHAPTER 22

The Friday after my return from Israel, the doorbell rang. When I opened the door, a slim man about an inch taller than my 5' 7" stood on the porch. A jumble of blonde curls, deep-set bright blue eyes, and a wide smile greeted me. "Good morning, I'm Tom Lott," he said, extending his right hand. As I shook his hand, a large furry gray cat ambled between our legs toward the front porch. "I love cats," Tom said emphatically. Our eyes followed the cat down the steps and out to the small white pebbles which covered my narrow front yard. I watched her quietly eat the dark droppings Madchen had left after breakfast. He was horrified. I explained to Tom that this was a morning ritual at my house. "I would get rid of that nasty cat!" Tom commented quickly.

After inviting him to come in and have a seat, I explained that the cat, Annias, belonged to my daughter, Sara, who no longer had the patience to put up with her advanced age. Then Tom stated the reason for his visit. He was looking for someone to proofread a book he had written, which had to be mailed to the publishers on the following Monday. The person who usually did this for him was not available. Having seen me walking Madchen on the road which led by his house, he offered to pay me eight dollars an hour for my help. I smiled and accepted the job.

Returning after lunch with the manuscript, Tom and I worked steadily the rest of the day and until 10:00 that night - with a short break for sandwiches which I quickly prepared. By the end of Saturday, we were making good progress, but it took all of Sunday to complete the job. Containing a collection of very short experiences that had happened during Tom's life, beginning with his birth, the book's appropriate title was *Snippets*.

Tom's house was a two-story house with a large deck winding around the right side and across the back. The back deck was high above an almost vertical wooded lot which descended to the road in front of my house. Constructed from gray weathered wood, windows on all sides let light into a large living room with a stone fireplace, several bedrooms, and a small kitchen. At the back of the living room was a six-foot sliding glass door - similar to mine. The one big difference was that the view from his porch encompassed many more miles of the same range of mountains. After my daughters had visited both houses, they would laughingly point out that Tom's view was much better than mine!

During the coming months, Tom would often come down for a meal and a visit. I would go to his house to watch movies he rented and play pool on the table he had in his basement. As we visited between houses, I learned that Tom had been born in New Rochelle, New York, thirteen months before I was. His father was a teacher in the local high school and his mother was at home. Tom's younger brother, Dale, was born four years after Tom. His mother had insisted that Tom take piano lessons when he was ten. Grudgingly leaving his friends and the baseball field nearby, he took lessons for six weeks. The seventh week, his teacher announced that on the following Monday, he was to meet at a local church for a recital. "What's a recital?" Tom questioned. "You will play this piece you have learned for parents, along with six other students of mine." So Tom unhappily appeared the next week and played in the recital. When he realized that he was the only boy in the class, he refused to return for another lesson. Today, Tom plays any Broadway tune by ear and I, after studying piano for three years in college, can only play what is written on the music in front of me! I also learned that he had been first a boy soprano in his church's choir and then later a soloist in the same choir until he was nineteen.

His musical accomplishments in high school were unbelievable. He had written words and music for the junior and senior musicals. During the four years he attended Columbia College in New York City, he would take his dates to Broadway plays on a regular basis. I soon began to feel that I had met someone else with a song in his heart.

After Tom married Joan in New Rochelle in 1952, he had taught math and science in high school for twelve years. Two daughters had been born to them during this time. One year he had taught in Morecomb, England, on a Fulbright Scholarship. They had bought a pretty two-story brick house in Hamilton, the home of Colgate University, wanting to raise their daughters in a university town.

Then Tom was exposed to computers through working at odd times in a computer lab near home. He felt that the computer was the perfect place for his love of science and math to come together. When he was offered the job of building a computer lab for an extension of the University of New York, Tom could not turn down the offer. Upon approaching Joan about a needed move to take the job, she refused. So they eventually divorced and Tom sadly relocated about seventy miles away. For the next twenty years, Tom did freelance software computer design for large and small New Jersey companies including IBM. Then he met and married Marty.

Tom loved to travel as much as I did, and he would decide on inexpensive ways to travel to foreign countries. In the summer that he finished teaching in Morecomb, England, Joan and Tom boarded a boat that sailed from Brindisi, Italy, and after visiting ports in Japan, India, Singapore, and Hong Kong, the trip ended at Yokohama, Japan. Other summers he had taken walking tours around Ireland as well as returning to India, and the northern parts of China and eastern Europe.

Three years before we met, Tom had come to Asheville after an amicable divorce from Marty. They had come south from New Jersey in 1983 to settle in Savannah. There they had purchased an old duplex in the historic section of Savannah. Marty was interested in antiques and restoring old houses. Finding Savannah too hot in the summers, they had relocated to Clayton, Georgia. Here they remodeled a very large old residence which they converted into a well- located bed and breakfast.

Tom needed to make repairs to the half of the duplex in Savannah which was for rent. So in the middle of January, we packed his Ford van with tools, paint, tennis racquets, and other things we would need. The balmy coastal air felt good after biting winter winds in the mountains. Each morning was spent making needed repairs. Then we would head for a nearby restaurant and the tennis court. Tom's skill with a hammer and saw made the basic repairs and my skill with a paint brush finished the job within the time we had wanted to spend. We both felt good about how well we worked together.

After we returned from Savannah, I was helping Tom repair some leaks in the basement of his house. Suddenly, I began to feel very strange as I watched him work. Could I be falling in love with this man who "wore so many hats?" When he stopped for a break, I shared my feelings with him. He looked at me soberly and admitted he was beginning the feel the same way. I had not even considered looking for a relationship more serious than a friendship. My one-person house was a happy place for me. I had even joined a community band in Hendersonville and was taking watercolor classes in nearby workshops. But I had to admit to myself that I missed being married.

When I realized that I was in love with Tom, I tossed and turned all night, wondering if I could really be in love so soon after David's death. David had told me that, if anything ever happened to him, he would want me to remarry. When I got up the next morning, I walked out into the hall leading to my living room. An apparition stood at the center of the hall. David, dressed in a long-sleeved white shirt – which he only wore on special occasions, stood – tall and handsome – smiling at me. In a moment he was gone. Was he giving me his blessing? I hoped so.

Tom had dated several women on a casual basis during the years after leaving Clayton, and had stayed busy with bridge club activities and traveling. On one occasion, when Tom went out of town on business, he returned very late at night. The morning after he returned, I found a note under my front door that read, "I wanted you to know I passed this way and reached out to your dreams. There will be some hard times in the weeks ahead, but I hope there will follow many weeks that will be ours alone to build a happiness that will surpass any that I have known. Thanks for your touch in my life. He works in mysterious ways, but knows it was meant to be."

I wanted my girls to meet Tom. If they did not like him, I would not even consider a serious relationship with him. I had told him of my life with David and he had seen pictures of all the girls and their families. Sara invited us to Decatur to meet Chuck, Hannah, and Joseph so they could get to know him. We also stopped by Jennifer's and Tommy's farm to have lunch with them and meet David and Daniel. I had a hard time waiting until I got back to Arden to get a report from this branch of my family! They seemed attracted to his jovial spirit, so I relaxed.

In March, I sent Kelli a copy of *Snippets* to read before we drove to Gaithersburg, Maryland. She greeted us warmly. While we ate lunch, I casually asked if she had had a chance to read his book. Kelli looked squarely at Tom and said, "Well, there was a mistake on the first line of the third paragraph in the first chapter." Tom and I exchanged frantic glances as she continued, "The word that you used to describe your father's glance at you in the hospital means 'the top of a mountain.'" We all laughed heartily, realizing that the spell checker on the computer could not tell the difference!

When we returned to Arden, Tom's daughter from Wisconsin came for several days. I had invited them down for lunch and was trying hard to "put my best foot forward." The pie I had baked for desert filled the kitchen with a good smell when the doorbell rang. Standing a little taller than her father, Cathy's wide smile was surrounded by long, bronze ringlets. Her hazel eyes shone as she admired the view. Then she started humming, "Can she bake a cherry pie, Billy Boy, Billy Boy." I laughed and told her that my father had been Billy Boy in my family. Then I wondered if she was checking to see if I could cook! After lunch we visited in the living room. Cathy noticed my antique Lincoln rocker and looked surprised. "Did Dad bring his Lincoln rocker down here?" Tom and I looked at each other, thinking the same thought. We had matching antique rockers. Surely that was a sign that we belonged together!

Spring was particularly beautiful that year. My sister, Ricie, and her husband, Jim, had moved to Arden and lived within walking distance of my house. They both seemed to like Tom as we visited back and forth. Betty also enjoyed watching our relationship grow. I had checked in with all three girls and they could see my happiness with Tom. This was all that mattered to them.

A jewelry store in downtown Asheville went out of business and all of their jewelry was half price. Tom, who I was beginning to learn could stretch a dollar even farther than David, took me there to see if I could find an engagement ring. In the showcase, at the very bottom of a large group of diamond rings, I spotted a beautiful ring that had a small sapphire on either side of a diamond of the same size. My large hand needed a ring that was this style. So the jeweler kept it to size for my finger after Tom paid for it. At the same time, we picked out a matching white gold band.

When I questioned Tom about whether or not he wanted to wear a wedding ring, his blue eyes started to twinkle. I wondered what mischief he was up to. The next day we headed to Hendersonville where he knew of a good pawn shop. Now my curiosity was really growing. When he pulled out a gold ring from his pocket and asked the clerk if he had one of similar value, the clerk brought out one that fit his finger. I knew the rule was that I was to pay for his ring as he had done for mine. The clerk told Tom that he would swap his ring for the one he wanted. So I put away my wallet and we both left the store happy!

By now we were making plans for a wedding. When Tom had seen pictures of David and realized he was over 6' tall, he grieved. "How could you possibly want to marry a shrimp like me?" he told me on one occasion. His height had always been a sorrow to him. His brother, Dale, had inherited their father's 6' stature. On many occasions, he would comment that he got tired of looking up to a passing girl. I tried to point out the advantage we had of being able to wear the same size shirt or sweater.

There was one serious consideration that I did not realize until I had fallen for Tom. Our religious beliefs were miles apart. When we discussed who would perform the wedding ceremony, I insisted on a religious one, rather than a civil one. I knew of a couple living in Black Mountain who had been at seminary with us. Jack was teaching Bible History at Montreat College where

David and I had had a summer cottage many years before. Jack, Sylvia, his wife, and their daughter had been with me in Western Europe in 1982. With our differences, I was hesitant to consider a church.

While driving around Hendersonville, we had driven up to a park high above the town. It was called Jump Off Rock Park. From the stone slabs that were surrounded by a strong metal railing, you could look across a deep valley to Mt. Pisgah - one of the highest mountains in this part of the Appalachian chain. With our deep love of mountain views, we both felt this would be a perfect place for the ceremony. I contacted Jack and Sylvia, telling them of our idea, and more importantly, asking if Jack would be willing to perform the ceremony. They did not know about the park, but trusted our judgment. Because of the park's location and the fact that Jack could not give us a definite date for the ceremony, Tom and I decided to have the four of us go to the park for a simple ceremony early in July. In August, we would have a big party for all the family at the park, near our house on Mt. Royal.

After we had gotten the results of our required blood tests, Tom and I went to the courthouse to apply for the marriage license. We worked on writing the marriage vows. A recording of "The Holy City" sung by the minister's wife at the church Tom had been attending was to be used for the music. I picked out a simple linen suit and ordered a bridal bouquet of daisies. Wedding announcements were on hand to be sent at the appropriate time.

The usual mountain summer rains had started by the first week of July. I would anxiously check the weather report and watch the mist rise from the distant mountains. We hoped a morning wedding might miss the afternoon rains – but each day passed with no clearing. Finally, Jack called me and said, "Eleanor, it has to be this week, because I am leaving town next Monday." So on Thursday, July 13th, I called Jack and Sylvia and said, "Come on. Maybe by the time you get here and we get to the park in Hendersonville, the clouds will have lifted."

We put Madchen in her crate behind the back seat. Jack brought the notebook containing the marriage vows we had written, and we had the certificate of marriage to be filled out afterwards. Only that morning had I read the document and realized two witnesses were required in Henderson County. It was too late to get another person. I did not mention this to Jack and Sylvia, but Tom and I decided we could chain Madchen to the stone bench which was to hold the tape recorder. She would be our other witness!

Just as we reached the park entrance, the rain stopped and the sun shone weakly through the dripping trees surrounding the park. Sylvia had brought a camera to record the happy event. Jack stood in front of Tom and me while Sylvia stood on my right. After the playing of "The Holy City," Jack began the service. When the service ended, we started putting things away in the van. A tall man in hiking clothes and a young boy stopped us to ask if we were having a wedding. He offered to take pictures of the four of us while Madchen lay at my feet. Upon thanking him, I found out that he was on vacation and was the minister of the First Presbyterian Church of Miami, Florida. I secretly felt we had been doubly blessed – with two Presbyterian ministers in attendance!

The minute we had everything and everyone in the van, the skies opened up. We drove slowly down the mountain, and out the main highway to the restaurant I had chosen for our wedding breakfast. I was pleased when I discovered the menu was serving prime rib and wide choice of vegetables that day. After the table was cleared, Jack signed the marriage license, and Sylvia signed her name as one of the witnesses. I can't remember whether or not they noticed that another name was needed for a witness. I do remember carefully writing "Madchen Moylan" on the line for the other witness! When I reported to

Sara that Madchen had been the other witness, she exclaimed, "Mother, you are not legally married!" I replied calmly that I did not think anyone would know Madchen Moylan was a dog. She had to agree, and after fifteen years, we have never heard a word from the courthouse where the license was recorded.

Since early June, Tom and I had been looking for another house – realizing that his house needed a lot of repair and mine was too small for two people. We both wanted a house with a good view of the mountains. Nothing seemed to be suitable that was advertised in the real estate section. Betty was keeping an eye out for us, but she was not having any more luck than we were. Finally, Tom came home one afternoon and excitedly announced, "I think I have found the perfect place in Leicester." This is a small mountain community about fourteen miles from the center of Asheville. A local builder had put the one story brick with a full basement on a ridge at the end of a long valley.

We drove to the property the next afternoon, after finding out that the present owner was moving on July first. Knowing how much I liked surprises, Tom would not give me any description. When we turned off the main highway, he started slowing down and said, "Look at the name of the next street." I could not believe my eyes when the sign read, "Rainbow Ridge Drive." Turning onto the private road, we passed a large house on the right and another smaller yellow brick house as we rounded a wide curve up the short hill. Directly in front of us was a tall metal fence with a large, ornate gate. I gasped, "Is this a cemetery?" Tom said he did not know. The house for sale was fifty feet below the gate on the left hand side.

A narrow front porch extended from the double carport. The dark red brick house faced the street, and was surrounded by a hillside covered with apple trees on the right. Anxious to see the inside, we rang the bell. The lanky dark-haired owner dressed in overalls welcomed us. We entered a short hallway which led into a narrow living room and dining room area on our right, and three bedrooms and two baths on the left. A red-brick double fireplace was on the back wall of the living room and the bedroom directly behind it. We stepped down into a large family room, after looking at the narrow kitchen. Six-foot sliding glass doors filled the back wall of the family room. We could not believe our eyes when our host opened the doors onto a small back porch with wrought iron railings, and beyond it, the valley Tom had seen previously. I sat down in an old fashioned white slat swing at one end of the porch and began to swing as I looked toward four receding mountain ranges. The owner pointed to 6,684 foot Mt. Mitchell on the far left. I suddenly realized we were looking at the highest mountain east of the Mississippi River!

After seeing the downstairs which contained space for another bedroom, furnace, laundry room and work bench, we were ready to make an offer. With Betty's help, we sold both of our houses and purchased the Rainbow Ridge property by the middle of August.

We set the last weekend in July for all the family to come to Arden for our wedding celebration. Mt. Royal had a large covered picnic area complete with a fireplace and refrigerators which we reserved for that Saturday afternoon. There were eight picnic tables near the fireplace end and room enough to put a serving table by the refrigerators. We even found a four piece band that provided music during the supper and dancing afterwards. Ricie's eighteen-year-old son, Bill, was hired to provide sandwiches, punch, fruit cups, and a decorated cake large enough to feed the twenty guests. Tom's two daughters flew into Asheville – Cathy from Wisconsin and Betsy from Boston. Sara and Chuck came from Decatur as did my long time friends, Winnie and Ann from Atlanta. Kelli flew into Atlanta, and rode up with Sara and Chuck. After supper, which included cutting the wedding cake in the "traditional" manner, we danced and visited until 8:00 p.m. Then Tom's daughters and my daughters got to visit longer in my living room. With Sara playing familiar songs, we all joined in. Thanking everyone for coming to make this a memorable event, goodbyes were said.

Hearing foreign languages spoken has always been "music to my ears." My two years of teaching in Ecuador added to this pleasure. So when Tom and I decided on Italy for our two-week honeymoon, I jumped at the chance to learn Italian. The set of Berlitz conversational tapes gave me all the common phrases I would need. You can imagine my delight when I found many of the Italian words were similar to the Spanish.

This similarity got us into trouble only once during our trip. When making reservations for a bed and breakfast in Florence, I told the owner that we would be arriving on the twelfth. When we opened the door, the owner threw her apron over her face, exclaiming that we had been expected two days before. She graciously found a large closet into which she put a mattress for that night, and made better arrangements for the rest of our visit!

Going by train south from Rome, we visited famous historic sites such as Mt. Vesuvius. But I thought going into the Blue Grotto on the Isle of Capri was unbelievable, especially when the small boat's oarsman began to sing "O Sole' Mio" while our eyes got accustomed to the ice blue reflection of the cave's bottom. That was eclipsed, however, when the blue-green tiny waves came skipping across the canals of Venice.

My real estate friend, Betty, had worked miracles with the two buyers of our Arden houses and the owner of the Rainbow Ridge property before we left for Italy. We managed to have all three closings within a week. Before the ink was dry, Tom had secured local movers to move both houses the week after we returned from Italy. Friends and family gathered around to help us pack. When Tom was undecided about moving the pool table, I voted a hearty "yes," thinking of how much fun my grandchildren had already had when visiting his house. The large family room at Rainbow Ridge was perfect, and not only did we all enjoy games, but a cat that later became a welcome part of the family would chase balls toward the pocket. As the balls which she could not rescue disappeared below the surface, her bewildered look gave us a good laugh.

# CHAPTER 23

Our move to Rainbow Ridge from Arden went very smoothly. When the moving company found that a pool table was in the load, they added a fourth person, thinking it had the usual heavy stone plates in the bottom. Upon loading it from Tom's house, they discovered the very manageable top separated from the base with attached legs, so there was no weight problem. It was the first piece unloaded when they arrived and fit perfectly at one end of the large playroom. The charge was by the hour, and because each pair could be working at the same time, the entire load was finished before lunch.

Tom and I found that there was no room for the small yellow and white kitchen table and chairs I had used in Arden. The large picture window on the mountain side of the narrow kitchen needed a table and chairs from which to enjoy the never-ending light changes during the day. So while I began to unpack, Tom started designing a four-by-eight-foot extension that would fit between the side of the back porch and the double glass doors leading into the third bedroom from a narrow wooden porch. Having all the skills necessary to build this, he was well on his way.

At the end of our first week, I walked down the driveway and across the street to meet our closest neighbors. The tan frame one-story house with a long sloping driveway seemed as friendly as the round smiling face of the older woman who opened the door. "I am your new neighbor, Eleanor Moylan," I announced as I extended my right hand. "Come in, come in," she responded, "My name is Jane." Passing through a large kitchen area, we entered an attractive family room with floral chintz covered sofas and a wing chair circled in front of a large red-brick fireplace. After exchanging information about our families, Jane asked, "Do you sing?" Smiling enthusiastically, I reported that I had been singing in church choirs since the age of twelve. "My church is the Bell United Methodist Church which you can see below my front porch!" Jane continued, "We would love to have you join our choir. We practice at seven o'clock on Wednesday nights." I admitted that I had been a Presbyterian all my life, but that being able to walk to choir practice would be good exercise as well a chance to sing. Bidding her good-bye, I invited her to come over to see our view.

As I started out for the grocery store the next morning, I paused long enough to admire the small dark red-brick church with the tall steeple and beautiful narrow stained glass windows, located on the corner. Over the next eight years, many happy hours would be spent in fellowship with the members of this church. Having spent my first ten years in these same Blue Ridge Mountains, I was well aware of how history had traced the Scots who had come to settle in the hollows of these same mountains.

When I was putting up our mailbox at the bottom of our hill, I noticed the name "McIntosh" on the adjoining mailbox. Looking to my right, I could see a corrugated tin roof above a one-story farm house between the trees. My curiosity led me to the front door and, after several loud knocks, a short rotund grey-haired figure greeted me. "I am your new neighbor on Rainbow Ridge," I said. "My name is Dixie McIntosh," she responded with a wide smile. I jokingly retorted," So you are one of the Scots who came down this valley!" Dixie invited me into the kitchen where she was shelling beans and told me all about her family. This visit was the beginning of a long friendship.

When Thanksgiving weekend arrived, four cement footings had been poured for the corners of the addition. The corner posts were in place and one outside wall had been completed by the time Sara, Chuck, and their children, Hannah and Joseph, had arrived to cheer us on. The big surprise was the pink enamel two-person Jacuzzi Tom had ordered to fill the remainder of the eight-foot addition. Another picture window, the same size as the one in the kitchen, had been installed for the benefit of anyone soaking in the Jacuzzi. Several years later, Tom converted a basement closet into a small, full bathroom off the narrow bedroom which held a bunk bed. This area was put to good use when the grandchildren came to visit.

Number Eight Rainbow Ridge Drive would see family members and friends come to exclaim over the extensive view. Lisa and C.J. came to visit by themselves when their parents were attending overseas dental conventions. One spring afternoon, I heard big "Oh's," as I saw them witness the first flight of two baby bluebirds leaving the bluebird house for the tops of thick bushes a few feet below. Shining eyes and wide smiles looked my way as I invited them inside for milk and cookies.

The next Fourth of July found the four Stowes and the five Bohannons filling every chair around the dining room table. Tommy and Jennifer had adopted a three- and-a-half-year-old girl from an orphanage in Latvia. The small stocky girl they had named Dasha was a little reticent when her parents introduced her. The long golden curls hung sideways when her solemn wide blue eyes looked carefully at her new grandparents. Hannah and Joseph ran out to the two apple trees on the side hill to see if the spring blossoms had changed to tiny green apples. David and Daniel adjusted the cue sticks with Tom's help and began a lively game of pool. Sara and Jennifer got the ice cream churn ready for the ice cream to be "making" while we ate lunch.

Later in the afternoon, the watermelon was served on the back porch. I noticed that the grandchildren were teasingly spitting the seeds on each other's plates. "Let's have a contest to see who can spit the seed the farthest," I announced. Five giggling children stood in a straight line at the porch's opening toward the back yard. Tom and Tommy stood where they could see where each seed had landed. After each round, the winner was announced amid loud cheers. When both families had left to return to Georgia, Tom and I watched the fireworks which were visible in three places from our porch, the middle ones coming from downtown Asheville.

The following Thanksgiving all three of the girls and their families gathered for the holiday weekend. Dasha had become comfortable with Tom and me and the house that had so many fun things to do. While the girls were helping me get the dinner ready, Tom organized a fifty-yard race on the paved road directly in front of the house. David, Daniel, Joseph, and Dasha stood in a straight line, eagerly watching Tom. Holding a small flag above his head, Tom blew the whistle, and the race was on. Dasha's short stocky legs moved like pistons as she easily beat her brothers and cousin.

Sara and her family and Jennifer and her family were expected for Christmas in December. Several days before they arrived, Madchen had refused to come out of her crate when I called her for breakfast. For several months, I had noticed that she was losing the strength in her back legs. She had led such an active life for thirteen years that I was saddened by this weakness. When I coaxed Madchen out of her crate that morning, I noticed she had not been able to control her bladder. With a heavy heart, I realized that this was not the life she wanted to live. I called the vet that had been taking care of her and explained the situation. When we arrived the next morning, he agreed with me. A big part of my heart followed her down the hall – knowing I would never see her again. Christmas for the whole family was saddened by her death.

Two years later, Sara brought me a ball of yellow fur which was about ten weeks old. She knew how much Tom loved cats and how much we missed Madchen. This was the smallest kitten in her cat's last litter. Bringing bowls and blanket, food and even a toy, I could not refuse to make Rainbow Ridge her new home. But upon close examination, Tom and I could not determine whether the kitten was a he or a she. Wanting to give it a name, we decided to call the kitten "Sandy." That way, the name would be suitable for either sex. When Sandy was ready for the first set of shots, the vet answered this question. Sandy was a definite "he."

Wanting to make life easy for Sandy and for us, Tom installed a cat door in the wall beside the sliding glass doors leading to the porch. It did not take long for Sandy to be trained to go outside. He really preferred the grass and enjoyed watching the humming birds come to the feeder which hung from the porch rafter. When we ate a meal, Sandy would patiently wait at the kitchen's entrance for a taste of spaghetti sauce – this was his favorite. A morning ritual was his coming down our long hallway to wake us up when he was hungry. Jumping onto the bottom of our antique rope bed, he would make room for himself between our shoulders.

Sandy seemed to take a personal interest in anyone who came to call. The bright green eyes would look intently at each person. But when Tom and I returned from an errand and found the painter, whom we had hired to repaint the family room's ceiling, standing near the top of a six-foot wooden ladder with Sandy wrapped around his neck – that was the last straw! The painter explained that Sandy kept trying to climb up the ladder after him. Finally, this was the only solution he could think of.

When we called for Sandy to come in for supper on Halloween Eve two-and-a –half years later, he did not appear. The next morning came and no Sandy. We called all the neighbors, visited the animal shelter several miles away, and checked every ditch along the highways. We finally gave up, thinking that some car had stopped for the light, seen Sandy wanting to get in, and had opened the door. We were reluctant to get another cat. Not only did he never have an accident inside the house, but he never jumped up on the counters or tables.

There was a small community center near our house on Rainbow Ridge. Every Fourth of July there would be a big barbeque dinner for the purpose of raising money to make improvements at the community center. One day I noticed someone had built a tarred walking path of exactly one mile on the ball field in front of the center. My mother had instilled the healthy benefits of regular exercise. Now my doctor had taken up the idea. So once a week, I would put on my walking shoes to do the circle at least one time.

One morning, I noticed a younger woman in front of me. A little more than 5' tall, her long dark straight hair would swing as she kept a steady pace. When she finished her walk, I sat down beside her and introduced myself. I learned that Vicky had been brought up in New York, moved south when she had married, and was the mother of an active six-year-old boy named Tim. I told her a little bit about my life up to this point. I told her of my wish for someone to help me improve my ability to play the flute. Her dark brown eyes flashed with excitement. "Oh, I play the flute myself!" she exclaimed.

When I found out that she lived in a trailer park nearby, I invited her up to our house to play duets with me. I discovered that she had a wonderful tone and taught flute lessons when someone wanted them. I also discovered that at the age of eight, Vicky would lead bird watching groups in her home town. When we sat in the swing on our porch, she would interrupt our conversation with the identification of a nearby bird song that I had not even heard!

At choir practice the next week, I asked the choir director about the possibility of playing duets during a church service. Karen was delighted and before long Vicky joined me on a Sunday morning.

Neil was the minister at Bell United Methodist Church when Tom and I moved to Rainbow Ridge Drive. Soon after I started coming to church, he knocked on our front door. I was happy to introduce him to Tom and show him our view. Although Tom was not a regular at church, Neil and Tom became fast friends. Neil's warm handshake and wide smile would always greet Tom when he attended church. His Christmas Eve service was a particular favorite of Tom's and mine.

When Tom found a bridge group in Asheville, he played on a weekly basis. I found out through a friend that Meals on Wheels needed a substitute who could deliver meals in our area when the regular person was not available. Tom and I enjoyed getting to know the different roads winding through the mountains as well as the people who were so grateful for a hot meal. Another advantage that larger Asheville had over Arden was a house for senior citizens. This was centrally located on a residential street. Many activities such as exercise classes, lunches on special occasions, and ballroom dance classes were held here. I learned t'ai chi here, which was a great help with a continuing balance problem. Tom had also joined a writer's workshop that met there. The thirty-minute drive from Rainbow Ridge encouraged us to combine our schedules whenever possible.

Through the alumni association of the college from which I graduated – which was now Presbyterian School for Christian Education - I had discovered that Martha, who had lived on the same dormitory hall with me, was living in Asheville. She and her husband, Henry, lived around the corner from the Senior Citizen's Center, so I would stop on a regular basis to swap books we were reading and catch up on family news.

Since David's death in 1992, I had dreamed of taking the girls and their families to visit Ireland. His great grandfather had sailed from Cork to the United States during the potato famine in 1868. When a travel agent showed me a folder advertising Mallow Castle, it looked like the perfect home for a large family vacation. I knew it would meet all our needs. I called the three families and we decided the Easter Week of 1999 would be just the right amount of time needed. The reservation was made for Mallow Castle, and each family hurried to get tickets and passports for each person.

When we landed at Shannon after a comfortable overnight flight, Rich, Tommy, Clif, and Tom hurried to rent cars suitable for each family while I enlisted everyone else to help get the luggage organized and ready to load into the cars. The first night we stayed at the airport hotel. It was the first time any of the grandchildren, except Dasha, had flown overseas, and everyone needed a chance to adjust! The next morning we drove two hours southeast to the small town of Mallow. The good directions we had received from the castle owners brought us to a large, ornate iron gate. Following the winding driveway, our four cars came to a stop at a two-story gray stone lodge. This originally had been the stables for Mallow Castle. In our anticipation, no one noticed the ruins of the castle among the trees. It had been burned many years before when King Charles I of England had marched through Ireland. The lodge was surrounded by acres of farmland which included a working dairy. We could see small deer grazing in a nearby pasture.

The owners greeted us warmly and helped us get settled on the second story of the west wing. Here there were bedrooms and baths for Tom and me and the three families. As I came down the curved stairway, Mrs. Allen led me into a large living room with a huge fireplace on the back wall. Three tall narrow windows were on the opposite wall. This room led into a long narrow dining room which held a banquet-size dining table that would seat sixteen people. She explained that we would be served an evening meal at 7:00 and breakfast every morning at 8:00. That left the days free for our families to sightsee within driving distance of the town.

Each family had made plans to visit neighboring famous landmarks. Kelli and her family all got to kiss the famous Blarney Stone on one of their trips. During time spent on the estate, the grandsons would wander around the pasture. One afternoon, David came running with a discarded antler from a deer. Before the week was over, each grandson had his own "trophy."

Thursday was chosen for the whole family to drive to the seaside town of Cork. All of us were anxious to see the port from which David's great-grandfather had sailed. Inside the visitor's center we could watch a video which showed the torturous crossing. Even five-year-old Dasha admitted that watching the ship on the tossing waves made her seasick.

The high point of my trip to Ireland was my visit to Trinity College in Dublin. Here was displayed the original Book of Kells – a very famous Irish treasure. I had the replica at home, but the original was beyond my imagination.

On the following Saturday, we packed our bags and thanked the Allens for a holiday all of us would long remember. Driving back to Shannon, the rental cars were returned and we took our places in line for boarding. Ahead of me were the four grandsons, each one with a deer antler protruding from his backpack.  I had to smile as I noticed puzzled glances from several fellow passengers.  These boys would have a good time showing their friends this souvenir from Ireland.  Many fond memories filled our thoughts as we returned to Atlanta.

One of Tom's favorite bridge partners was his first cousin, Betty, who lived in Orlando, Florida.  Beginning in 1997, we became "snowbirds" – spending one or two weeks of January and/or February in Orlando.  David's mother's second cousin, Helen, also lived near Betty.  Helen and her son, David, lived in a stucco house with a small yard.  The flower beds by her front porch were awash with orange, purples, and yellows every time I came to visit.  The first three winters we stayed with Betty.  The next two years we lived in a condo of our own in Wimbledon Estates which appropriately had wonderful tennis courts.  Friends and family came for long weekends to enjoy trips to Disney World and many other attractions.  Three of my Cotopaxi colleagues, Pam, Nellie, and Janet came one long weekend in February of 2001.  This was the first reunion we had had since leaving Ecuador many years before.

Bridge was one of Tom's favorite pastimes.  The other was walking around Walmart.  In Leicester, he had to drive twelve miles to the nearest one.  But in Orlando, there was one within two blocks of our condo.  While I would be trying to get the light just right for a water color painting on which I was working, Tom would spend a happy hour there.

When Tom and I realized we were not able to rent the condo during the remainder of the year, we sold it.  But we continue to go to Orlando each winter to visit Betty, Helen, and David.  Betty is happy to have a bridge partner.  I spend many happy hours visiting museums and painting the unique trees and flowers found in the area.

On my return from an African trip, I noticed I was having trouble standing when I sang in the choir.  Thinking that I was just tired from our travels, I did not worry. But when this problem persisted, I checked with a neurologist in Asheville. He could not find anything to cause this. Remembering the excellent reputation of the Emory Clinic in Atlanta, I contacted the head of the neurology department there. I discovered from the examination that I had orthostatic tremors-a very rare condition. Medication seemed to help, but I decided to sit in a back row instead of stand in the choir loft. Now, many years later, I still take medication for this and have to make sure I have something to hold onto when standing in lines.

I met Bobbie soon after we moved to Rainbow Ridge. Now Bobbie and I were regulars on the back row. Both of us had come from Presbyterian backgrounds, but we officially became Methodist on the Sunday we joined the church. When Bobbie found out that Tom and I played bridge, we would drive several miles north to the large wooden house they had built, and join Bradley, her husband, and Bobbie for many afternoons of bridge. We also joined them and their visiting family for holiday dinners.

Alice was another church member that I visited quite often. Her knowledge of plants would see me through my poor attempts to start new varieties of house plants as well as different ways to fix hamburger! Now, over twelve years later, Bobbie and Alice still stay in touch with me – even though we live in different states.

In the spring of 2002, Tom decided he had had enough of driving fourteen miles one way to play bridge. The mall where his bridge game was held faced Tunnel Road, a main road on the south end of Asheville. We looked at the city map and located the nearest residential area to this part of town. When looking in the telephone book for the number of Sally, a long time friend, I happily discovered she lived on Chunn's Cove. This was the street facing Tunnel Road at the mall. Next door to this mall was a Walmart! So I hurriedly called Sally and asked if she had seen any FOR SALE signs in her neighborhood. After explaining the reason for my question, she excitedly responded," Yes, there is one house right around the corner from me that has a 'For Sale By Owner' in the front yard."

It was Sunday afternoon, so Tom and I drove into Asheville to the address Sally had given us, hoping to find the owner at home. The one-story red brick house was in a small neighborhood on the side of one of Asheville's many hills. The owner welcomed us and gave us a tour of the three bedrooms, two bath house. Directly behind the living room was a long kitchen and small dining room. The six foot sliding glass doors in the dining room opened to a small wooden deck which faced a fence. A double garage opening in to a full basement looked ideal for the furniture and other things we needed to move from the basement on Rainbow Ridge. The owner was being transferred at the end of the summer. His asking price was negotiable. So Tom offered to draw up a contract contingent on the sale of the Rainbow Ridge house.

We returned home and immediately started thinking about the move. We called an ad into Asheville paper the next day. The lawn service had the exterior well-kept.

When prospective buyers came, we would start by walking to the back yard to see the view. We laughingly told one person that the house was selling for a thousand dollars and the view for a million. By August, we had said goodbye to this view and moved the pool table one more time to the large basement room on Chunn's View Drive.

Before Tom and I had left Orlando in January, I began to have severe pain in my right hip. When I went to see a specialist while we were there, she discovered that the progression of arthritis had caused the cushion that separated the hip's joint to disappear. Bone was rubbing on bone! With the help of medication, I was able to make it through the move, but as soon as we were settled, I made an appointment with an orthopedic surgeon. In August, the hip was completely replaced. Thanks to excellent rehabilitation, I have been pain free since then.

# CHAPTER 24

Betty and I wanted to try another overseas trip. My brother, E.K., a pilot for Northwest Airlines, recommended a travel company owned by his airline. When we contacted them, they were just beginning to advertise a trip to four cities both of us wanted to visit. These were Hong Kong, Bangkok, Singapore, and Bali. We had read just enough about each one to be excited – especially when we heard the cost.

The travel company offered two nights and one half-day tour in each city. We wanted to spend a full two weeks, so we added two more days to the last three cities. Leaving on February 1st, 1995, we flew directly to Singapore after refueling in Tokyo, Japan. I lifted the shade of my window just high enough to see the glittering white snow on the side of Mt. Fuji.

Betty and I saw interesting animals in an island zoo across the bay on the half-day tour in Singapore. The next day, we walked around the city famous for being so clean that you would be arrested for throwing down used chewing gum! The botanical gardens there had giant orchids in bloom and rows of other tropical plants which you could smell for a long way. Our third day of the tour, we flew to Bangkok, arriving just before midnight. The travel agent was standing outside the baggage area, holding a large sign high above his head. We cheered when we saw our names on the sign. Thirty minutes later, we arrived at a seven-story hotel facing the wide river which bisects this huge city. During our days in Bangkok, we enjoyed watching the traffic on the Chao Phyaya River.

A high point of our two weeks was the day trip we took to see the bridge over the River Kwai. Betty had longed to walk on this bridge, since the movie made it famous. The small museum and cemetery held sobering memories of the battles fought there. Another day's tour took us to the original capitol of Thailand. I am afraid that we really got tired of taking our shoes off before entering the twelve temples. But the ornate Buddhas and designs inside the temples were very much worth the effort.

The long flight to Bali, gave us time to catch our breath from the bustle of industrial Bangkok to the easy-going island life of Bali. Tropical heat greeted us the minute we left the terminal with our gracious, small, dark-skinned guide. Picking mid-priced hotels for our tour, each one had been modest, centrally located, and had provided very adequate service. When the tour guide opened the door of our car in front of the hotel in Bali, we felt as though we had entered a magical world. The large two-story wooden structure had big round posts holding up curved balconies in the front and the back. We walked between rows of tropical flowers bordered by palm trees. The dark cool interior was welcome. We picked up our room keys, and made our way to a room which faced the gray-green waters of the Indian Ocean.

Changing into lighter-weight clothes, we walked down a winding staircase that led to an open courtyard. Small tables were set for dinner around a large bonfire. We relaxed over a simple supper of fish and fruit before turning in early. The guide was picking us up at 8:00 in the morning for a full day.

During the next day's tour, we left the city streets, and drove on narrow, curving roads that led through winding, low lying hills. We passed narrow terraces of rice that looked like geometric designs from the air. At one stop, native workers were carving beautiful wooden bowls, flower arrangements, and candle sticks. Farther up the hill was a batik factory – open for tourists to watch the intricate process of multiple dye bath needed for the multicolored fabrics. Banana trees lived on both sides of the road.

The last day I discovered that snorkeling equipment could be rented at the hotel. While Betty read, I quickly changed and hired a guide to row a small boat off shore to look for coral. As I swam slowly above I found that the angular reef was not as distinctive as what I had seen in Australia, but the experience was worth writing about in my diary!

The last four days of our tour were spent in Hong Kong. The first day was spent on the island, visiting famous markets, and riding the trolley to the hotel on the top of Mt. Victoria. The leisurely walk back down led us through a botanical garden with exotic plants in bloom. The day before we flew home, Betty and I boarded an "airbus" ferry for the two-hour ride across the Pearl River Estuary to Macau – the mainland city of China that still belonged to Portugal. After lunch we rode north to visit the city where Sun Yet Sen lived; he was president of China for only one year.

Betty had gone to Africa after we returned from our trip with Northwest Travel. She was so enthusiastic; I wanted to experience this also. Tom was more than willing to go, since he had not seen this part of Africa. So in the spring of 1996, we signed up with a British tour group for one week in Kenya and one week in Tanzania. The small group of twenty met us in Nairobi, the capital of Kenya. During the next week, we saw many native animals in their natural habitat. The two small white safari jeeps in which we rode had open tops, making it possible for us to take pictures of the lion family that was in no hurry to get out of our way. Cheetahs watched us warily from large rocks high above us. The elephants would let us get within touching distance! Hundreds of pink flamingos lifted, all at one time, from the shallow waters of the large lake just before we got to the Masa Mara.

We crossed the equator at one point, and stopped to admire the rugged peaks of Mt. Kenya. The second week found us at a very comfortable lodge in north central Tanzania. From here, we drove to the edge of the Ngorongoro Crater. The next two days, we left the lodge early to drive down steep winding roads to the bottom of the crater. Elephants, rhinos, and smaller native animals would cross our path during the day-long trips. The large alkaline lake at one end of the crater's floor attracted hundreds of greater and lesser flamingos. On leaving the crater of the last day's tour, we finally spotted the elusive leopard, lazily stretching his yellow with black spotted body over a low lying limb of a tall tree. Our guide kept a cooler of bottled water in the small jeep, as the heat and dust from the unpaved roads made us very thirsty.

One new experience for me was the hot air balloon ride at dawn over the Serengeti Plain. At about five hundred feet, we could see herds of elephants moving in the early morning. When you are riding, you feel like you are levitating above the earth with no effort. There is no wind because YOU are the wind! Consequently, there is total silence.

During the final drive back to Nairobi, the clouds lifted and we saw the shining snowy peak of Mt. Kilimanjaro. The perfect end to our African experience, the tour group agreed.

Tom had wanted me to meet his aunt and first cousin who lived in Wales. Since our flight to Africa changed planes in London, we decided to spend two more weeks in the British Isles. I was happily surprised to find it only took two days to drive to Wales. Tom had made arrangements with Chris, his first cousin, to spend the second night with him and his family. We met his wife, Sheila, and enjoyed an evening at a Welsh pub where we went for supper. The next morning we left to drive northwest toward Edinburgh. I had seen the high, rugged mountains of this part of Wales in movies. But rain had already started as we bid Chris and Sheila good-bye. The fog was so thick as we drove the first part of the morning, we could not see any of the scenery to which I had looked forward.

Reaching Edinburgh around 4:00, we found a small bed and breakfast on Prince Street. Both of us had been to Edinburgh before, so sightseeing was not on our list. To our delight, the hostess told us there was to be a chamber music concert that evening within walking distance. An excellent chamber music group gave a very interesting program. The next morning we drove south through Scotland to Oxford, England, with a short stop to see the new cathedral in York.

While sightseeing at Oxford, we saw an advertisement for a current play in London. Entering the shop, we were delighted to find that we could purchase tickets for two days later. Leaving Oxford the next morning, we drove to Heathrow Airport outside of London and got a room at the airport hotel for two nights. After turning in our car the next morning, we boarded the 9:00 train for London. Here we spent the day visiting the famous Haymarket in the morning and going to the matinee performance of the Neil Simon production in the afternoon. The return train stopped near a restaurant where we had supper before turning in early. We were exhausted! The flight back to Atlanta left at 9:00 a.m.

The spring of 1997, Betty swapped her timeshare in Gatlinburg for one on the Costa del Sol in Spain. We landed in Madrid, the capital. Here we spent two days visiting the world famous Prado art museum and having supper at one of Ernest Hemingway's favorite restaurants. Then we took the fast train south to Malaga on the coast for a week at the Doña Lola Club.

The condo was well equipped with ever thing we needed for our visit. Beautiful pools for outdoor as well as indoor swimming, tennis courts, and a dining room overlooking the sparkling blue waters of the Mediterranean were available. From the main office, we could book day tours to surrounding towns. Wanting to make every minute count, Betty and I took a tour to Granada, the site of the world famous Alhambra, the first day. Never before had we encountered architectural style and beauty as we found there. Another day we drove high into the mountains where we visited a small goat cheese factory. This had been a family business for over one hundred and fifty years!

The tour we took to Tangiers, Morocco, however, introduced us to a whole new world. Our experienced guide warned us before we arrived about pickpockets and the relentless peddlers on the narrow streets of the city. The restaurant where we lunched had long Oriental rugs hanging on every wall. Before we left the city, we took an hour to visit a park where camel rides were given. I got no farther than being seated on the wide leather saddle before my churning stomach forced me to dismount.

The last two days of our trip to Spain were spent in Seville. Here again the famous cathedral proved to be an architectural wonder. We rode an elevator to a lookout on the top, from where we could see the city sprawled in all directions. I found the Castilian Spanish spoken in Spain, with its beautiful soft "th" sound, did not keep me from understanding the language. My South American Spanish was different but very helpful.

Tom did go to Spain with me, accompanied by Eunice and her husband, Rhea, as well as Winnie and her husband, Paul; I had bought a condo when Betty and I were there the year before. This time, Tom and I decided to extend our vacation a few days by driving up the coast to Barcelona. After two days of sightseeing, we caught the midnight train back to Madrid for our return to Asheville. As we were waiting for the train to arrive, I was sitting on the cold concrete divider with my head resting on my arms. I suddenly heard an American's voice saying "I hear a voice from North Carolina!" A tall, slim brunette was coming our way.

Jumping up, I replied, "Yes, we are from Asheville." Holding out her right hand, Laura introduced herself. She was glad to have company on the late train. When we arrived in Madrid, she came with us to our hotel to see if there was another vacancy for her. Finding none, we promised to meet her the next morning. During lunch, we discovered that Laura's father owned a condo near Asheville. The next summer we visited her at his home and met the rest of the family. Today, many years later, we still exchange Christmas cards.

The year after the family went to Ireland in 1999, Tom and I saw an ad by Grand Circle Travel in Boston that was going to China. At that time, the Three Gorges Dam was still under construction. It had been many years since Tom had been to Beijing, and he was anxious to see the changes. I had always wanted to see the Great Wall.

From the very beginning, the trip was well organized and well handled. One feature with a travel company I had never experienced was a visit in local homes. Our group was divided into small groups, each of which would eat a meal with a family. After being divided into groups of five, the group Tom and I were in rode in two rickshaws which bumped over the narrow cobblestone streets to a neighborhood close to our hotel. This neighborhood consisted of city-built narrow apartments in two-story brick buildings. We knocked on the red wooden door, and were warmly greeted by the grandmother and her daughter. With halting English, the grandmother told us they rented the apartment. We enjoyed a simple lunch followed by non-verbal conversation that included a lot of pointing to art work, family pictures, and scenes nearby, to which we responded with understanding smiles. They were obviously proud to be living in this nice apartment.

After driving out to see the excavation of the Terracotta Warriors and the Great Wall, we drove south to board the cruise ship for the trip down the Yangtze River. Three days later, we stopped for lunch at the site of the Three Gorges Dam. My engineering genes really bloomed when I saw the mechanical wonders that were being performed by the hurrying workers. We bid goodbye to China ten days later from Hong Kong – a city Tom and I both consider to be one of our favorites.

I was so impressed by Grand Circle Travel that when Betty called me about a trip they were advertising to Eastern Europe in October of 2001, I was definitely interested. Warsaw, the capital of Poland, was our first stop. We were surprised at how many historical events had taken place there.

The next main city we visited was Krakow on the southern border of Poland. Here we visited several interesting buildings and sites, all relating to Jewish history. When we crossed the border into the Czech Republic, we were stopped. We had to give the authorities our passports and stand outside the bus while it was being inspected. Finally, we were admitted and got back our passports.

Prague was our destination in the Czech Republic. While we were waiting for our group at the St. Charles Bridge, we happened to get a chance to see President Carter. When he saw our group, he stepped out of the black limousine, and came around to hand a long-stem American Beauty rose to one of our group. He must have just arrived after flying all night, because he looked very pale.

After several days there, we turned west and flew to Vienna, Austria. It was all I could hope for – to see the tombs of so many composers I knew and loved. My favorite of all the tombs was Mozart's – with a blanket of bright red roses lying on the grave. While other members of our group visited the opera house, Betty and I watched the morning workout of the world-famous Lipizzaner Stallions. The building in which they are kept had a balcony from where we could see the small gray bodies with swinging white tails stepping in perfect rhythm as they went through their routine. Our horse-loving daughters were delighted with the pictures we brought them.

Before we left Vienna, we drove outside of the city to visit the home of Beethoven. My heart did sing, as I stood in front of the house where he had written David's favorite – the Ninth Symphony.

In November of 2002, Betty and I flew to Cairo, Egypt, after joining the other members of the Grand Circle Travel tour at La Guardia airport in New York. Our group stayed in a Moorish style hotel on the east bank of the Nile River. During the week, the thirty of us were divided into groups of five to be taken to local homes for an evening meal. This gave us a chance to discuss local history, national events, and the opportunity to get to know our Egyptian hosts.

After the week there, we drove east to board Grand Circle's cruise ship for two more weeks' of sailing south on the Nile. Here we divided into two groups. Betty and I felt very fortunate to be assigned to the group which was led by the tour director, Nabil. He was a certified Egyptologist and he spent many hours sharing his knowledge of hieroglyphics with us. As his over 6' body stood beside the stone entrances to the temples, the dark eyes under the slightly wavy dark hair would be very serious as his long arms would trace the carvings which explained Egyptian names and places. The cruise ship took us all the way to the Aswan Dam, stopping during the day at famous temples and pyramids. The midday heat was oppressive, so we left the boat early – to beat the heat and the crowds of tourists.

At Luxor, a bus took eight of us to meet two hot air balloons at 6:00 one morning. The people in charge made sure we lifted off by 6:30 – just as the sun was rising. When we reached four hundred feet, we could see the Valley of the Kings to the west of us. Beneath us, the sun shone on a patchwork of crops growing on the narrow strip of land beside the west side of the Nile River.

My friend, Bobbie, from Rainbow Ridge days, wanted someone to go to Scandinavia in February of 2003. When Grand Circle Travel advertised that the trip would be preceded by a week in St. Petersburg, Russia, I was hooked. The first day after we arrived, we toured the palace of Catherine the First – the wife of Peter the Great. The gardens surrounding the palace were worth the whole trip! And the exterior is a marvel, with a row of white columns crowned with gold that grace the 300 foot long façade of brilliant turquoise. I added one more world famous museum to my list – The Hermitage. When I saw that it occupied the huge and opulent Winter Palace – a gilded one-thousand-room residence that was the home of six czars – I began to get tired!

Bobbie and I were disappointed that the famous Russian ballet at the Hermitage Theater was not giving a performance while we were there. We did, however, enjoy being driven into the country outside of the city, to have an early evening meal with a young couple on their farm. After greeting them, we went upstairs to a simple kitchen where the meal was on the table. Dishes of cabbage, meat, and artichokes were surrounded by slices of crusty bread and fruit. As we talked about our life in the United Stated and their life here – I looked out the window and could almost hear Cossacks riding across the open fields.

The next day we flew to Helsinki, Finland. There were people everywhere in the streets when we left the airport. Our tour guide announced that it was the queen's birthday, and we were going first to the palace to see her wave to her subjects. The courtyard in front of the palace was full of women and men in native costumes. One tall blonde lady with a warm smile asked me if I would like to hear about her costume. It had been made by her grandmother and worn by women on special occasions. After a marching band all dressed in similar costumes played for the queen, the crowds dispersed, and we rode the bus to the hotel. The next morning, we rode to the park which had a statue of John Sibelius, the Finnish composer. Up a grassy slope from the Sibelius Memorial was the Temppeliaukio Church, an amazing auditorium that was built into a mass of solid rock. I wondered how the acoustics were, but we did not stay long enough to sing.

Flying across the Baltic Sea, we landed in Stockholm, Sweden, where we felt as though we were floating - because everywhere we looked, there was water. More beautiful blonde ladies threw flowers in our path as we boarded the airplane for Oslo, Norway. Bobbie and I found attractive woolen sweaters and gloves for ourselves and as gifts for our families. Our next stop was Copenhagen, Denmark, where we spent several days enjoying local sights and historical monuments. Flying back to Stockholm, we spent one night at the hotel for a farewell dinner before flying home to New York. I felt as though I had been "around the world in eighty days." But whether or not I am traveling abroad or here, I agreed with Dorothy in "The Wizard of Oz," that there is no place like home.

# CHAPTER 25

Interaction with people has always brought me pleasure. Age, occupation, race, or physical appearance has never been a barrier. My mother told me that, at the age of five, I earnestly inquired about the health of a visitor's sister.

The only time I can remember being at a loss for words was at my seventieth birthday celebration. One daughter had planned a family gathering at the Grove Park Inn in Asheville. The beautiful mountain setting, the outstanding array of food, and the group of family and best friends made the occasion memorable. After the dessert, each daughter made a heart-warming toast to me. I was too full of pride and happiness to respond. Sara broke the silence with, "My mother is speechless!"

This was a first as my gregarious nature was common knowledge. The happy event had taken place the summer before our move from Rainbow Ridge to Chunns' View Drive. That August seemed to be hotter than usual. After the moving van had finished placing everything inside the house, Tom and I decided we did not like where the washing machine had been placed in a basement room. We were standing in the driveway, trying to decide about this, when a tall stalwart African-American and a short blonde with deep dimples came from across the street. "You look like you could use some help," the man announced, smiling broadly as he extended his right hand. "My name is Chris and this is my wife, Donna," he continued. Tom and I introduced ourselves, confessing that we had not made the right decision about where to put the washing machine before the movers left. Within a few minutes, the change was made and they left, making us promise we would call if they could be of any more assistance.

Our house was in the middle of the first of two blocks at the bottom of a hill. Another short street went up the hill to a second row of homes. Tom and I got to know the neighbors when we walked. Several families had been there a long time and filled our ears with tales about the bear who would come down the mountain and turn over garbage cans at first light!

Our next door neighbors were a retired couple who had lived in their home for thirty-five years. Charles was the Minister of Music at the large First Baptist Church of Asheville. While I was recovering from my hip replacement, Mae and I would swim in a therapy pool at a retirement home in downtown Asheville. Every Monday morning found us meeting at my car or hers to go for this swim.

Tom and I loved the location of our new house. The grocery store, Wal-Mart, his bridge group, and good restaurants were within a five minute's drive. The Blue Ridge Parkway was almost within sight of Chunns' View Drive. On the Parkway was the Folk Art Center. This had rotating arts and crafts exhibits, as well as a shop which carried a variety of jewelry, linens, pottery, and other local crafts.

I wanted to start painting again, using the instruction I had gotten at the workshops in Arden. Here at Chunns' View I had a studio to work where I could leave my "works in progress." Our

British friend, Eunice, a painter with thirty years of experience, and her husband, Rhea, lived close enough for me to join her for painting. Her expertise was invaluable as she guided me in making paintings for friends and family.

I had had back problems before. After we moved to Rainbow Ridge, I discovered Dr. Mike. His experienced hands would release any hidden "kink", giving me instant relief. His dark brown eyes would always show concern about any issue I had, physical or otherwise. Dr. Mike continued to treat any back issue I had until we moved to Georgia. Being careful not to lift anything heavier than I can carefully pick up, I continue to have no pain.

When coming from the mall near us one day, I noticed a long, narrow building with a simple white cross on the roof. A glass and metal sign near the building advertised Tunnel Road Associate Reformed Presbyterian Church. When I visited the next Sunday, a small congregation welcomed me. I joined soon afterwards, and was glad to return to my Presbyterian roots.

The church was a converted motel that had several rooms behind the large front room for the sanctuary. One was a church office and two were Sunday school rooms. When I joined, the congregation felt that there was no room to grow. So they began advertising and within six months, a company who wanted to put a large hotel on that corner, offered the church a very good price.

The church relocated to West Asheville and held Sunday morning services at the VFW hut. We voted to change the name to New Beginnings Presbyterian Church, since we were no longer located on Tunnel Road. John became the interim pastor when he and his wife, Betty, joined the small congregation. He brought us inspiring sermons and Bible studies. These expanded our knowledge of the Bible, and our spirits grew even if the size of the congregation did not. Elspeth provided the music as well as keeping our finances straight. Many months were spent looking for a permanent home for New Beginnings. But with a change in the pastor, the original congregation either moved away or found other church homes.

This same group, however, would meet once a month in Martha's home. Elspeth, Mimi, Ann, Luttrell, Katie, Phyllis, and I would decide on a study guide which was of interest to everyone. After one hour of study, we would meet around the dining room table to enjoy lunch and more fellowship.

When Martha and her daughter, Kay, had to move back to Concord where Martha's family could help take care of her, the group moved to Katie's and Phyllis' house on the same street. Katie insisted on serving delicious desserts and drinks to go with the sandwiches each of us brought. Now, three years later, the members still gather. Mimi and I have moved away, but others have joined the group.

Asheville has one of the best nature centers I have seen anywhere. I bought the family membership which gave me access to visit any time it was open. The grandchildren would ask to go there first on every visit. Each time we went, the animals and birds would keep them entertained for several hours. The outdoor cages for red wolves, a male and female panther, and several other large animals were in natural settings on the side of the mountain. On the lowest level, we could watch a small elephant stretching his trunk out to pour water over his body.

Vicky, my flute-playing friend from Leicester, joined me here on several occasions. At other times, she would come to help the workers with particular problems with birds. One worker, Carlton, called on her frequently when he could not get a wing to mend. She had told me about Carlton before, so I was not surprised when she announced that they were going to be married. They picked the botanical garden at the University of North Carolina's Asheville campus for a lovely, small, outdoor wedding. Six of the members of the flute ensemble from her church provided the music. We helped her sell her trailer after she had moved to Carlton's small log house at Horseshoe after the wedding. I was happy that Tim had a step-father now.

Just below the Nature Center on the same hillside, Asheville had a recreation park. We brought the grandchildren here to ride on the small merry-go-round, the roller coaster, and to swim in a large tiled pool. On the occasion of Lisa's eighth birthday, I surprised them all by announcing that I had had a birthday party and had gone swimming in the same pool when *I* was eight!

When I wanted to visit acres of trees and flowers, I would drive west across town to the North Carolina Arboretum. If I got tired of walking the well-kept paths, I would go inside a two story building that was filled with art or craft displays such as quilts. Every season of the year except winter, the beauty displayed here made my heart sing!

Betty, my travel partner, was helping to raise money for the Literary Council of Buncombe County. She called and said, "I am going to kick you if you don't volunteer as a reading tutor at the Literacy Council." When I called to see about this possibility, I was delighted to find there was a training class starting the next month. The director of the program soon called me to meet with a forty-two-year-old student who had come to them for help. She introduced me to Salerna, a short stocky African-American girl with wide dark eyes and a broad smile. After hearing details about my background as a reading teacher, Salerna said that she would like to be accepted in the program. My job was made easy by the fact that I could meet with Salerna in the office of the apartments where she lived a five minute's drive from Chunns' View Drive and a wealth of materials in the council's library.

At our first session, Salerna confided that she was tired of being called "retarded." On checking her file, I found that she had finished the tenth grade at a special school in Asheville that taught only the "mentally challenged" – my word for this problem! Her eagerness to learn was a joy. During the next two years, I saw her reading level advance from a low second-grade level to a solid fourth-grade level. She had been married, but her husband divorced her soon after the birth of their only child – a son. The mother, who lived nearby, raised the boy. Salerna had suffered with epilepsy in former years, and this qualified her for a weekly disability check, which covered her basic needs. But her personal goal was to be able to get a job to earn more money. With the help of counseling through another agency in town, Salerna was able to obtain a part-time job with Goodwill Industries in Asheville. She worked hard on her math skills, but could neither multiply nor divide. Several years later when I asked what she did on her job, she happily announced that she helped count the different items that were donated. This job gave her the extra money that she wanted.

At this time, arthritis in my right hand had affected the last two fingers, so I was no longer able to reach all the notes on my flute. In a desperate search for something I could play, I happened to hear the clear beautiful sound of a string at the July craft fair in the Civic Center. Upon investigation, I discovered it came from a bowed psaltery, and immediately bought one. Having played the cello, I was happy with another string instrument. I continue to enjoy the singing tones of a one-line melody.

On one of my morning walks in the neighborhood, I noticed activity around the house two doors from me; it had been empty for a long time. As I passed the driveway leading up to the red brick house built very much like ours, a tall woman with short gray hair and wide dark eyes raised her hand in greeting. I walked up the driveway, and introduced myself as her neighbor. Gerry's broad smile encouraged me to tell all about myself, before I realized I was not giving her a chance to do the same. She and her husband, Bill, had just moved into the neighborhood, wanting to be close to their daughter, who lived nearby.

We became fast friends, and spent many happy hours exchanging recipes, walking their beautiful Golden Retriever, Sandy, and crying on each other's shoulders over our disappointments. Tom and I thought we had talents, until we met Gerry and Bill. She made award-winning wreaths out of dried leaves and other interesting parts of trees. Bill was a master with wood, duplicating any piece of furniture or any item. Their appreciation for antiques helped me to decide what to do with an antique dresser I did not have room for, when we moved two years later. It now compliments a matching antique bed in their guestroom!

My brother, E.K., called me from his home in Hawaii in March of 2005. He felt that it was time for all of the Whiting family to have a reunion. After researching possible places on the east coast, he had found a state park outside of Greenville, South Carolina, which had a lodge and seven cabins on a small lake. It could be reserved for a group of forty or less people. The kitchen was supplied with two large refrigerators, two large stoves, and all the dishes, pans, glasses, and silverware needed for forty people. I decided I would help him with the arrangements, and he would do all the contacting of family who would be coming from six states including Hawaii. We were overjoyed when we discovered that all the cabins had linens and heat for cool mornings.

The second long weekend of June found my brother and his wife, Marianne, and all four of us sisters with our families, as well as E.K.'s son and daughter with their spouses, gathered for this happy event. "Accompanying" Kim and Jeff, his daughter and son-in law, were the newest additions to our family – twins – Izzie and Ben, who were going to be two in August. Everyone took turns fixing simple meals and cleaning up. But most of all, visiting with family members some had never met, made the weekend a great success.

The next winter, we visited Tom's cousin, Betty, in a retirement community in Orlando. This community was owned by a national company that had built fifty-seven others using the same plan, located all over the United States. When we returned to Asheville at the end of February, Tom and I began to think seriously of making the same move Betty had. He had never liked to do yard work, and I was getting tired of all the space we thought we wanted three years before. In addition, an Asheville developer had just finished building twenty small homes, creating a fully developed street parallel to ours. For a year, we had listened to large trucks rumble by to complete this project; our neighborhood was doubling.

Tom went to the computer, and found the exact duplicate retirement community in Athens, Georgia. We called and made an appointment to see what Iris Place Retirement Community had to offer. When we arrived the next week, we were delighted to find there were small cottages built on a curving drive in back of the main three-story building. Betty's community did not have room for cottages, so this feature was a bonus for us. There was nothing available at this time, so we put our names on the waiting list. As we left Iris Place to drive back to Asheville, I noticed a Walmart within a short distance. Quickly, I looked to see if Tom had also seen the store. His wide smile answered my question.

I tried to rationalize the move from my favorite mountains, by thinking on the fact that six of my seven grandchildren were already in college. If I was going to be a part of their lives, I needed to be closer to them. Athens seemed like the perfect distance to visit these two daughters and their families. Sara was still living in the neighborhood near where she had grown up in Decatur. Jennifer had been living on Tommy's family's farm in Winder – twenty miles away. The University of Georgia is located in Athens, where three grandchildren were enrolled as students. When I thought about the advantages a college town provides for lovers of art and music, I did not feel any regret about the decision to move.

I called Helen, a former neighbor in Arden, to tell her of our plans to move to Georgia. She told me that they needed a double bed for their guestroom. "Yes," I replied excitedly. "We have an antique rope bed that might be just want you want." As soon as they could find a time to come over, Paul, her husband, and Helen looked at the bed. She admitted later that Paul had been against the idea, but the minute he saw the bed, I could tell he was sold. After Tom gave them the history of the bed, Paul asked Tom for a large screw driver to take the bed apart. We settled on a price, and they loaded the bed in their station wagon. When Helen saw my sad face as they were leaving, she said," Now, when you come to visit us, you can sleep in your bed!" We have taken her up on her offer at least once since then.

When walking Sandy with Gerry one morning, I asked her advice about the best way to advertise our house. As we paused in front of the Mortenson's house, she exclaimed," Bob and Ann Marie are looking for a house just like theirs, but with a full basement." I had been in their house and found the floor plan to be identical to ours. Their garage, however, was on the same level. I called them after supper, and they told me they had already heard we were moving. On the following Saturday, they came to look over the house. With little hesitation, they said that they were interested. Tom had had many years of experience with real estate transactions, and offered to write the contract after we agreed on the price. Jean, a real estate broker who lived across the street from Bob and Ann Marie, was not happy, however, when she heard we had sold the house to them.

Bob's lawyer agreed to hold the closing, which was held the end of April. Tom offered to hold the mortgage. This worked to our advantage, because the payments Bob made every month paid for half of the rent at Iris Place.

During the first week of June, my sister in Columbia had fallen and sustained a concussion. All the family members that could come rushed to Columbia to be with her and Gay, her daughter. Connie had been living with Gay and her family since the death of Bill, her husband, twelve years earlier. Not able to stay long, most of us returned to our homes, only to come back on June 19th to say goodbye for the last time. She was buried next to her husband, Bill, in historic Quaker Cemetery in Camden, South Carolina, alongside our parents.

Wanting my Quito friends to see Asheville before we moved, Pam, Janet, and Nellie flew in for the last weekend in May. We started the visit by having lunch at the world famous Biltmore Estates. Anywhere I had traveled abroad, people would mention this place when I told them that I was from Asheville. When we first moved to Arden, I bought an annual family pass, which well paid for itself, as I brought other friends, as well as family, to see this estate which was built in 1893. Another landmark we visited was the Grove Park Inn, where I had celebrated my seventieth birthday.

Tom's daughters, Cathy from Wisconsin and Betsy from Boston, had come in the early spring. They enjoyed the ride up the Blue Ridge Parkway to see the banks of pink and white azaleas in bloom on each side of the road. Cathy, an avid gardener, insisted on buying clematis to plant around the base of the lamp post beside the curving walkway to our front door. Because I did not want the color of the bloom to fight with the dark red brick of the house, I chose one with a white bloom.

She felt her efforts were rewarded when I reported beautiful delicate white star-shaped blossoms before we moved.

In July, the Literacy Council of Buncombe County awarded me the signal honor of being voted one of the two most outstanding volunteers of the year. I had taken two more students after Salerna left the program. Now I was spending at least two hours a week tutoring Bea and Jerome. Bea was a sixty-two-year-old grandmother who had very limited reading skills. Jerome, at forty-five, had to begin with first-grade level books. By the time we moved to Athens, Jerome was fulfilling his desire to read from his Bible during church services. This was a happy ending to this chapter of my life!

By the middle of June, Iris Place called to say a cottage would be available on August first. We moved into high gear. We called Robert, a member of my church who worked for United Van Lines, to see if he would be available to move us. Tom and I realized we would not have room for the pool table, the bunk bed, three bookcases, and two sofas! When Robert came over to see what we wanted moved, he suggested renting a large U-Haul truck and moving us on his day off. This would save us money and give us more flexibility for deciding which day we would leave Asheville.

The three girls arrived during the fourth week in July to take any family items they could use. When Sara walked in and saw I had not started packing anything in the kitchen, she threw up her hands, knowing she did not have time to stay and help. Gerry and I discovered a new neighbor across the street had just finished unpacking all her china, and had trash bags filled with packing paper waiting for the garbage man. Sally, my friend from our Rock Hill days, called to offer to pack all the kitchen items. With her help, we soon had everything in boxes and ready for Robert.

There were many goodbyes to make to the friends who had become special. Ron and his wife, Ffife, had walked by one afternoon about 4:00. Four o'clock tea was a ritual at our house. That particular afternoon, Ada, their two-year-old pixie, with shoulder length brown hair and eyes to match, was swinging between them. The minute Tom saw them, he dashed down the driveway, holding two round sugar cookies out to Ada. From that time on, he was known as Cookie Tom! Benny, a member of our church, lived on a nearby street. He had received head injuries in Vietnam, and was living by himself in his mother's house. Many times I would take a dish of macaroni and cheese over for his supper. During many long talks our friendship grew, and I still hear from him at Christmas.

A retired couple from Chicago had moved into a "house in progress" as Harry would describe their one-story house at the bottom of our hill. His wife, Jean, had been a reporter for the Chicago Tribune, and kept writing projects going even then. Harry mostly wrote editorials to the Asheville Times. In these he would decry the building of all the new houses. "I moved here to get away from this sort of thing," he exclaimed in frustration. Jean died the year after we moved to Athens, but I stop by on return visits whenever possible.

When we were notified that a cottage would be available, Wanda, one of the managers, offered to measure the space in the living room and two bedrooms, so I would know which pieces of our furniture would fit. The living room had a fireplace on the back wall. Large corner windows gave good light. Tom's black Yamaha electronic piano would fit perfectly along a side wall. The garage had space for a large storage cabinet as well as the long table I used for my art projects at Chunns' View, and the small kitchen did have room for the large microwave we had recently purchased. Tom had to sell a very old dining room table which had been in his family, however.

After moving to Asheville, I was fortunate enough to be able to travel extensively. During my travels, I collected musical instruments, carefully picking one from each country. My first instrument had been the didgeridoo from Australia. I had to personally transfer this between flights all the way back to Asheville - it was considered a weapon - and, being made from oak, was certainly heavy enough. I had brought several instruments back from Ecuador including bamboo pan flutes and a charango, a small guitar with the body made from the shell of an armadillo. This I had brought back to my grandson who can play any guitar or banjo. Other instruments I collected were a toy balalaika from Russia, pipe flutes from Turkey, Israel, Ireland, and an ancient string instrument from Egypt resembling a mandolin. All of these instruments, except the charango, are now in the classroom of a music teacher at AB Tech in Asheville. He happily introduces them, including the country from which they came, to his beginning music classes.

Saying goodbye to the towering mountain foothills and the cool mountain air was the hardest. But knowing that we would be only three hours away was comforting. As I made my last round of goodbyes, I repeated, "I don't say 'Goodbye,' I say,' Hasta la vista.' " For those who don't know Spanish – it means "Until we see each other again."

# CHAPTER 26

When Tom and I pulled into Iris Place Retirement Community, we drove to our cottage. Robert followed with the truck. Then I went to the office of the main building to get the key. Linda and Charles were there to welcome us. Linda told us that supper was free for our family and friends for the first two weeks. That sounded good to me, as Sara and her family were coming over from Decatur to help us unpack. Linda and Charles had been on duty when we came to look at the cottages in April. Their helpfulness and genuine concern about all our needs really convinced Tom and me that we were making the right decision to move to Iris Place.

While the truck was being unloaded, I saw a car pull up and park beside Tom's white Kia in front of the cottage. A couple dashed toward me as I was crossing the front yard. After introducing themselves, Flo apologized for coming at such a bad time. She continued by explaining that they had just moved out, and had forgotten the bird feeder in the back yard. In the conversation that followed, Flo told me that she was an artist, and how good it had been to have the wall space in the cottage to hang her paintings. Bidding them a hurried goodbye,

I secretly hoped that living in the same space as an artist would inspire me!

After Robert and his helper got through unpacking the truck, I paid them, and thanked them for the good job they had done. They had to return to Asheville the same day, so we bid them goodbye.

About ten minutes after they left, Sara, Rich, Hannah, and Joseph arrived. Hannah unpacked all the hanging clothes that were stacked to the ceiling in the Subaru. Rich helped Tom set up the computer, and get all the heavy boxes opened for the rest of us to unpack. Sara started in the kitchen, and had the dishwasher loaded before I could turn around. They were used to the August heat, but I felt as though I could not breathe every time I went outside.

I heard a shout from someone across the street. A short slim figure was waving her hand and motioning for me to come over. When I went over, Doris introduced herself, and said she had cold lemonade for the whole family. I was overwhelmed at the hospitality of someone I had never met. I accepted gratefully and when I returned the glasses the next day, Doris had made us a plate of biscotti which was delicious when dipped in hot tea. Not knowing that Tom and I had tea every afternoon at 4:00, she could not have made a more appropriate welcoming gift!

Our monthly rent at Iris Place included all maintenance, as well as weekly cleaning service. In addition, a daily main meal gave Tom and me a chance to get to know the residents who lived in apartments in the three-story main building. There was always a manager and an assistant manager on duty twenty-four hours a day, seven days a week. The kitchen staff planned and provided well-balanced meals. Although Tom and I had retired from our jobs more than ten years before, we had had to do all the necessary household jobs. Now, when anything broke down or needed replacing, a call to the main office would bring Barry in his forest green truck to our doorway. Standing over six-feet tall, his lanky frame would have to duck as he came into the cottage to see why I called. When he finished, he would cheerfully remind us to call again when anything else was needed. Tom and I found out what real retirement was like!

When we went down the hill to the main building for lunch, Tom and I would sit with two other people at one of the many round tables which filled the dining room. When there was room, we would join Ray. While waiting for the food to come in from the kitchen, I would have time to discuss the many musical topics that were of interest to both of us.

Ray had started playing the piano several years earlier than I did. His mother was the organist at their church. So he naturally drifted toward the organ. His mother let him discover the many notes and pedals necessary to play the music he heard.

We kept learning about places where our paths had crossed. Ray taught organ for many years at Agnes Scott College in Decatur, Georgia. This was close to the neighborhood where I had lived for thirteen years. On another day, I found out that Ray's daughter had married the son of a trumpet player who had been with me at Transylvania Music Camp in Brevard, North Carolina, during the summer of 1951.

On Monday afternoons, Ray would play the piano during the hour when I sang with the Iris Place Singers. Our leader, Lois, would ask questions about the origin of some hymn or song. Ray would always come up with an answer. Often, he could expand the information with stories or other ideas that would give us all pleasure. Frances, who had been at Iris Place for many years, also accompanied us on the piano. She could play any hymn or popular song by ear. We were always grateful for these two outstanding musicians.

Sue, who also sang with the Iris Place Singers, heard that I was a Presbyterian. I gladly accepted the offer she made to come by every Sunday morning and take me to Friendship Presbyterian Church. Here I found people in the Sunday school and morning worship who welcomed me. Kathie would sit with Sue and me during the worship service. During the few minutes we had after the service, we would swap concerns and details of our activities from the preceding week. The stimulating discussions in Sunday school and the inspiring music during the worship services made my heart sing! Sue had a real gift for growing flowers. She made a garden on the hill above the main building. Here, these flowers bloomed spring, summer, and fall. She would share them with everyone, when she placed them in a vase at the entrance to the main building.

J.C, the activities director, showed me albums that were available to new residents that told about people living at Iris Place. I began to feel at home when I read about the lives of people who had been places I had. All of these albums were filled with attractive pictures and short histories. Kitty, the resident photographer, made each couple or individual come alive on these pages. I was constantly amazed at how many residents had had long and interesting careers.

Joy, for, example, had been a reporter for the Associated Press. On one of her assignments, she interviewed Maurice Chevalier – one of my favorite actors. At the end of the interview, he had leaned his tall frame over her four- foot slim form and planted a kiss on her cheek! When these people had retired, or while they were still employed, they traveled all over the world.

We were given a calendar of events on the first of every month. I soon learned why most of the residents, who were ten to fifteen years older than Tom and I, acted as though we were all the same age. Every morning, afternoon, and some evenings were filled with activities. The list included exercise programs, games, trips to interesting places, celebrations around holidays, and times for church services. Groups from organizations, as well as individuals, would come to Iris Place to enrich our lives.

From the time we moved into the cottage, our next door neighbor, Martha Jane, was available to give me information I needed. She gave us the name of her family doctor, Dr. Robert Aherns, as well as her dentist, Dr. Mark Shackleford. Painting and bird watching were two interests we shared. Martha Jane's helpful critique of a painting I had in progress would send me home with new ideas to try.

Athens has a very active art association which meets on a monthly basis. There I got acquainted with other artists, who told me about events at The State Botanical Garden of Georgia. Martha Jane would call me to tell me when the first humming birds arrived in the spring, or come to pick some flowers from the colorful flower bed behind her cottage. Her grown children reflected the same warmth and interest their mother had whenever they visited.

Sam lived across the street from our cottage. He lived alone, and when the weather permitted, we would walk with him down to the main building for lunch. When I saw Sam starting out, I would call Tom, and tell him it was time for us to go also. Even when it was raining, I would watch for Sam's car to pull out of his parking place. We would catch up on family news or any news of local or national importance on these walks. The Bradford pear trees line the driveway to the front entrance of Iris Place. When they bloom in the spring, these blooms looked like cotton balls floating among the branches! When I tried to make a pastel painting of these trees, I discovered that the white pastel was perfect to use for the blossoms. To make a balanced painting, I included the end of Sam's cottage. The result was very gratifying. When I showed it to Sam, he wistfully said he would like a copy. I was happy to give him the original. His daughter thanked me profusely, and his friendship has meant a lot to Tom and me.

Susan lived in a cottage near Martha Jane's. She was one of many friends I came to know and admire. Her watercolors of flowers were in a book she had illustrated that I had seen in the gift shop at The State Botanical Garden of Georgia. Also, there are two glass cases which display creations Susan had shaped from dried leaves, seed pods, sticks, and the remains of bugs. One group looks like Cinderella riding in her pumpkin on the way to the ball!

In the spring of 2008, Betty, my travel buddy from Asheville, and I decided to go to South Africa for three weeks. My main reason for going to South Africa was to visit Victoria Falls. I wanted to add another of The Seven Wonders of the Natural World to the list that had I started when I went to the Great Barrier Reef in Australia. The water descends 328 feet to the flat river basin between Victoria Falls and a matching cliff across from the falls. It was everything I could have hoped for, especially when rainbows appeared in the mist rising above the falls. While there, we visited several countries and saw wonderful wild life. On our day trips, we would look at "wild life" nearby – after getting tired of straining to see the head of a giraffe a mile away.

One afternoon, I suddenly spotted a large rhinoceros beetle that was not moving on the sandy strip beside my path. Stooping quickly to pick it up, I discovered it was not damaged. Thinking of Susan and her exhibit at The State Botanical Garden of Georgia, I took it back to her.

Betty gave me a sturdy box in which I could pack the beetle. When I presented Susan with the beetle, she explained, with a gleeful look, that it was a female rhinoceros beetle, because it did not have the big horns that identify the male. Her being able to tell the sex of the beetle amazed me.

Any time I had a problem or a question, I could depend on Susan to interrupt her busy schedule to help me. Her cornflower blue eyes beneath a rim of curly hair would sparkle as we talked.

Dorothy had come to live at Iris Place six months before Tom and I arrived. She was in charge of the prayer service on Wednesday nights. When I came to these services, I would sit on a front row seat, where I could join in the singing of favorite hymns. Dorothy's intense blue eyes under a rim of white curls would twinkle, as she welcomed all who came. Her remarks that followed prayers were an inspiration to me. They reflected a deep faith and extensive knowledge of the Bible. I always left with hope about some problem I was having.

I had always wanted to join a book club, but had never had the opportunity. When Dorothy invited me to join the one at Iris Place, I accepted happily. She would lead the discussions at our monthly meetings. Her grasp of ideas showed me that she would delve deeply into anything she was reading. Having retired from a long teaching career near her home in Plymouth, Massachusetts, Dorothy's love of learning was evident.

Two months after we had moved in, the doorbell rang one morning. When I opened the door, Elaine greeted me with a wide smile. After she introduced herself, we got seated at the dining room table. "Part of my job at UGA is directing the Ageing and Physical Performance Laboratory. I'm looking for volunteers from Iris Place to help us determine the level of physical activity Tom and you get from living in a cottage." With my love for exercise, I nodded my head quickly, and agreed to be a volunteer. Tom, with a little less enthusiasm, also volunteered. Elaine returned after the program was over to thank us for helping make it a success. This began a strong, lasting friendship between Elaine, her husband, Carl, and us.

I later found out that Elaine also organizes and leads workshops in many parts of the world. As many as twenty or thirty health professionals attend these meetings. For larger groups, she takes as many as four trainers with her. The trainers may be physical and occupational therapists as well as exercise physiologists – some of whom have doctorates in their fields. The people who attend these workshops come from Israel, Spain, the UK, Germany, Switzerland, Italy, and Scandinavia, as well as South America and Australia. We have had a good time trading travel experiences!

In July of 2007, I went to visit Tommy's mother, Mary, who lived at Mulberry Grove, an assisted living facility in Statham. As we talked in her room, I could tell she was unhappy – particularly with the food. When I told her about the meals at Iris Place, she couldn't believe how much better they were. The next Saturday, Mary came to Iris Place for lunch. She was so impressed that she had her son get in touch with Wanda to get an application for an apartment here.

She moved in six weeks later and introduced herself as Mary Bo, because there were several residents already with the name of Mary living on the first floor. When Tommy and Jennifer came to visit, they could visit both of us at the same time.

My doctor strongly recommended that I take a therapy yoga class that was offered at the Mind and Body Institute at Athens Regional Hospital, Continuing trouble with my balance convinced me this was a wise decision. At the first session of the class, Judi gave me a chance to go over all the issues I wanted to address. I was delighted to find an exercise class that could meet my needs. Each Tuesday morning I would leave the class "a new person!"

In August of 2008, my orthopedic specialist replaced my left knee. I had physical therapy in the pool at Athens Regional Medical Center for a month beforehand. This strengthened my leg muscles, so the recovery period would be shorter. By the middle of December, I was able to terminate the outpatient physical therapy, and return to therapy yoga.

I was getting discouraged with my efforts at watercolor. Martha Jane suggested I try my hand at pastels. Palmer, one of the residents at Iris Place, was recommended to me as a good resource. I told Palmer of my interest when Tom and I ate with him in the dining hall. His hazel eyes lit up! His gray mustache moved rapidly, as he told me that he would be happy to get me started in this medium. Several days later, I knocked on his apartment door. I could not believe what I saw. Beneath his front window stretched a long table that held a tall table easel. There were cabinets behind his easy chair, piled high with drawings, books, and art supplies. His walls on three sides had pastel paintings he had done over the years since he had retired. I knew I had found a gold mine. What made this gold mine so special was the fact that Palmer guided me on what pastels were the best to buy and what kind of paper would work. In addition, I left with three books on how to produce paintings I would treasure.

What I appreciated about Palmer the most, however, was his willingness to share his wealth of knowledge. The Christmas before we left Iris Place I received a notice from The Pastel Journal telling me that a year's subscription would be starting in January – compliments of Palmer!

By November, I felt confident enough to offer Sara and Rich a pastel painting of their dog, Buddy, a basset hound and beagle mix, with large, round, soft brown eyes that matched the markings on his shoulder and back. The white body and long tail were fun to paint, and it made a nice addition to their gallery of "family" portraits.

Iris Place was similar to the one in which Tom's cousin lived in Orlando, FLorida.   Anyone who lived here could stay in another facility for up to seven days free. This included all three meals. When we went to visit family and friends in Charleston, South Carolina, we made arrangements to spend a week there. During this week, we not only had good visits with several of David's family, but also took tours of interesting places in the city.

On New Year's Eve, Elaine and Carl came over to help us celebrate. Having just returned from Italy where Elaine had done a workshop, they entered, with Elaine holding a bottle of wine in one hand and a small, but heavy, green glass bottle in the other. Elaine's big smile signaled us that the small bottle held something very special. As we drank our wine, she asked for a piece of bread and a small dish. Opening the bottle, she poured a small amount of thick golden liquid into the dish. "Extra Virgin Olive Oil that was pressed from olives yesterday at my friend's house in Italy," she exclaimed. While I tasted the oil on the bread, she showed us her camera, which had a picture of her friend pressing the olives. I had tasted olive oil all my life – but nothing could compare with the taste in my mouth at that moment!

On Valentine's Day, the dining room walls and windows were decorated with bright red hearts and cupids - complete with arrows. After supper, Tom and I returned to the main building, where a five-piece band was sitting in front of the small grand piano. An artificial dance floor had been placed in front of the fireplace. Everyone enjoyed two hours of dancing and refreshments, which were served at the surrounding tables. Tom does not have many chances to put on his dancing shoes, so he made the most of the evening – changing partners whenever I wanted to sit one out. We enjoy dancing every chance we get since our marriage in 1994.

# CHAPTER 27

We had heard from Gerry, our former neighbor, that Ann Marie and Bob had sold their house. So we were not surprised, when their lawyer called us in the middle of March, 2008, and told us we would be getting the balance of the mortgage that we had been holding. When we saw the amount of the check, we could hardly believe our eyes! "We really need to invest this in real estate," Tom said quickly.

The next week, Tom and I began to contact several companies, to see if there were any small houses close to Iris Place. There were some large subdivisions, but I was not able to find a house without stairs. I had gotten used to the one-story cottage we had at Iris Place and, at our age, steps would be a handicap.

Tom came rushing into the cottage the next week with exciting news. A new subdivision within three miles of Iris Place was building small one-story houses. On Sunday afternoon, we drove over to Park West Blvd. to see them. The first house on the right had an "Open House" sign in the front yard. When we entered, there were several people there. An attractive blonde came over to us and introduced herself. "I am Judy with Keller

Williams Real Estate Company," she told us, as she held out her hand. Tom and I introduced ourselves, and told her we were looking for a small one-story house to buy.

I was so busy admiring the shiny dark oak floors and the ten foot ceilings, I had a hard time listening to the information Judy was giving us. There were three bedrooms, two bathrooms, and a small living room which opened into a sunroom through wide curved arches. The afternoon sun streaming through the four windows in the sunroom made the yellow walls feel warm. The narrow back yard at the back of the house was identical to the wooded area we had at Iris Place. "Just the place to hang our bird feeders," I thought happily.

Judy pointed out several features that the builder had incorporated. One was the doorways which were wide enough to accommodate a wheel chair. This was of particular interest, because I had already made an appointment with the orthopedic specialist to schedule a knee replacement.

I also liked the very large master bedroom which would have room enough for my desk, dresser, and bookcase. The bathroom adjoining the bedroom had a tub in which I could place handicap bars. An alarm system had been installed which had a feature I had not seen since moving from my first house in Arden. The soft tinkle of bells would sound every time either the back or the front door opened – alerting me of someone's entering or leaving. Also, an automatic watering system had been installed with small fixtures placed at appropriate places around the yard.

Judy spoke to the agent who was on duty, and got a drawing of the subdivision and information which included the price. When Tom and I saw the price, we realized that the houses were almost the same amount as the check we had just received. We told Judy that we wanted to consider buying. The agent had given Judy pictures of several styles. But Tom and I told her that we were most interested in the model home. When she asked when we would like to buy, we said, "Now!" Realizing we were serious, Judy and the agent from the selling agency discussed the matter, and by the end of the week, a contract was ready for us to sign.

We gave Iris Place the required one month's notice, and made arrangements to move on May 27th. The fact that we were able to pay cash eliminated several things that would have delayed our move.

The return to wooden floors was my greatest joy. The carpet in the cottage had made my balance problems obvious. I felt as though I were walking on the deck of a moving ship. Because our cottage was only three hundred square feet smaller, our furniture fit perfectly in the new house. The third bedroom, which happened to be at the front of the house, became my studio and computer room. The long wooden table I had used in Asheville fit under the double front windows, giving me all the light I needed. The back wall had room for the computer desk, as well as the filing cabinets we used for our records. When I unpacked the kitchen items, I could not believe how many shelves were in the pantry closet. I was not surprised when I learned that the builder was a woman. The Andersen windows required half the normal time to clean. The GE range with the glass top and self-cleaning oven certainly made my jobs easier. The laundry room was large enough to hold all my cleaning tools and supplies and there was still enough space in front of the washer and dryer for me to sort laundry.

The arrangement of the bathroom off my bedroom continues to be a great pleasure. The walk-in closet adjoining the bathroom is large enough to hold all of my hanging clothes. When the seasons change, I just turn to the other side of the closet and reach for the dress or blouse I need. The alcove on one side of the closet has a row of shelves deep enough and tall enough to hold plastic bins, in which I can store out-of-season items.

On the closet floor beneath these shelves, there is room for our luggage. Convenience has top priority in this design.

Tom and I sat at our small round table, and watched the first humming bird discover the feeder we had placed in the narrow back yard. Then we were sure spring was on the way. A month before that, I was walking out of the kitchen and movement in the back yard turned out to be three young does walking in a line toward the woods behind us. "They have no place of their own," I grieved.

When we put up our eight-foot spruce Christmas tree in December, the ten-foot ceiling was perfect for larger decorations I had never been able to use. The Andersen windows held many decorations which hung from suction cups. I could not find any way to hang our wreaths on the round white columns which border the front porch, but one fit nicely on the outside of the window of my studio.

During the winter, I am very happy to have the double garage. Here my car remains dry and warm until I need to go out. I had broken my wrist at Iris Place the year before from falling in an attempt to scrape the ice off the front windshield. And my addled brain never seems to remember to put a blanket on the windshield at night!

I invited the two girls who live close to Athens to come for dinner on Easter Sunday. Hannah, who is at UGA, and Jennifer's Dasha joined us. After eating all we could hold, Jennifer quickly loaded the dishwasher, while Sara got her guitar in tune. For the remainder of the afternoon, we sang our favorites, accompanied by Sara and her guitar.

This Easter we had bright yellow and white daffodils blooming between the low bushes at our front porch. Elaine, our thoughtful friend, had called in late January, saying she had extra bulbs looking for a new home, planting included! Since I am no longer able to kneel, and have about the brownest thumb in the world, I accepted her offer gratefully. The next afternoon, Elaine, with bucket, trowel, and bulbs in hand helped me pick out five places to plant. I had longed for some color in addition to the green of the bushes and the tan of the house. Sometimes I think Elaine works overtime – thinking of perfect ways to make people happy!

The rent at Iris Place had included maintenance, such as replacing batteries in the smoke alarms. So it never occurred to me to mark my calendar for when this needed to be done here. One of our smoke alarms started loudly buzzing about 3:00 a.m. one Sunday morning. I called 911, not knowing what else to do. Three policemen came to the door almost immediately. My face turned red with embarrassment when I admitted we could not get the alarm to stop. Two of the men left, but one lanky policeman offered to help. After locating the offending smoke alarm, he realized that the small circular box was ten feet above him. He offered to get the twelve foot ladder from his truck. Gratefully, we watched him replace the battery, and bid him a sleepy goodnight.

I was very fortunate to retain the services of Marian, the worker who had cleaned our cottage at Iris Place. She usually comes the first Friday of every month. When the door bell rings, I can see her tall solid figure and the wide smile below the round dark eyes. Of Mexican descent, the lilting Spanish she speaks on her cell phone during a short conversation makes me homesick for Quito. After she finishes cleaning, the house smells fresh and ready for another month of busy days.

J.C., the activities director at Iris Place, made it clear that Tom and I would be welcome to come back for any of the activities we had already been doing. Instead of riding with Sue to Sunday school and church every Sunday morning, I would meet her there. Debra, the hairdresser at the beauty solon at Iris Place, continues to keep my thin hair looking equally as good as Donna did in Asheville. I return on Monday afternoons to practice with the Iris Place Singers. On Thursday afternoons, Tom and I play RumiCube with Lillian, Liz, Bea, Rita, and Audrey – a group committed to this fun game. I also try to attend the very inspirational prayer meeting on Wednesday evenings when possible. When I come for the monthly book club, Dorothy's storehouse of humor and new ideas on old subjects is always at hand, and her willingness to share, makes our friendship very special to me.

I continue to attend the monthly meetings of the Athens Art Association at the Lyndon House, a community art center. Flo, who had lived in the cottage at Iris Place before us, now lives in an adjoining neighborhood. A long-standing member of this group, we often ride together to the meetings.

At one meeting, I sat beside someone I had never met. After introducing myself, I found out that she was a new member. Upon further inquiry, I found out that she lived within a ten minute drive from our house. Doris was living in a one- story red brick house which had a full basement. After finding out that I was not doing much painting, she asked if I would like to join her to paint once a week. This was just what I needed. I discovered her full basement was big enough for both of us to lay out our art supplies. Each week, we would paint for an hour and a half – taking turns at picking our subjects. I had been unhappy with painting from photographs, as my paintings looked like the picture! Her free style was just what I wanted to try – and I left each week with a painting that made me happy.

Photography has been a passion with me for as long as I can remember. When we were living in Leicester I was able to catch a goldfinch perched atop the backside of a large sunflower blossom. The morning sun lit the soft yellow breast of the gold finch as the sun's rays brought several shades of yellow to the back of the sunflower's petals. In the background were the gray-blue of the mountain's ridges. This award-winning photograph now hangs on the wall of our dining area – a fond reminder of the mountains I will always miss.

An increasing number of friends at Iris Place have to use wheel chairs and walkers. It is amazing how they manage the activities that are listed on the bulletin board. Sue and several of my closest friends are in their nineties, but they continue to be "young at heart." I was particularly saddened to learn of Palmer's death recently. Last January, I received a notice that Palmer had sent me a year's subscription to "The Pastel Journal." This was one more way he wanted to share his love of pastels. When I learned from his son that Palmer had spent his career teaching in elementary and high schools, I was happy those students experienced his interest and concern, which meant so much to me.

Six months after we moved to Park West Blvd., the Johnson family moved in next door. When I went over to welcome them, the grandfather introduced himself as Choyce Johnson. I remembered seeing the name on a street sign off of the highway I usually take to visit Sara in Decatur. Naturally curious about this, I asked his daughter, Denise, to explain. The slim attractive blonde told me that her father had been County Commissioner of Oconee County for two terms. This was the way the county had chosen to honor him.

Our subdivision is within two blocks of Atlanta Highway. Going east, it becomes Broad Street, the main road going through Athens. When we travel west, thirteen miles later, the same road turns onto the street that is close to Jennifer in Winder. Tom and I are happy with the savings in time and gas.

The girls and their families continue to come for family gatherings. They are happy that I have a house that is so easy to maintain. With all of these advantages, Tom and I look forward to many years in our last house.

# CHAPTER 28

The first twenty years of my adult life held the usual events that go with raising three children. Until the "nest was empty," there were the normal victories and losses found in any household with three active daughters.

After they had built their own nests, my path took a different direction for five years. With professional help, I came to realize that I was able to give more to David, as well as to family and friends. The seven years after my return from Ecuador gave me the chance to build a new relationship. This sadly ended in David's early death – due to lung cancer. I miss the brilliant mind, the dry humor, and the deep devotion to family, friends, and God. Now after fifteen years with Tom, I feel that David's wish for my happiness has been fulfilled.

From the time the girls were in their early teens, Thanksgiving weekends found the family driving north to Roanoke, Virginia. For several years, we visited Jean, Fred, and their children, Fred, Jr., and Jean Stewart at the large, stone house which had been built in the early 1800s. This house had been Fred's parents' summer home. Being several years older than our girls, Fred and Stewart delighted in entertaining them while

Thanksgiving dinner was being prepared by Jean and me. On one occasion, an early snow found Jennifer, Sara, and Stewart riding horses in the pasture below the house. Today, many years later and since the deaths of Fred and Jean Stewart, Tom and I visit Jean and Fred, Jr. several times a year.

His younger sister, Sara, goes between New York City and Charleston, South Carolina, where her daughter and family live. Her only son, David, and his wife, Sue, are the proud parents of very active triplets, who just started first grade on the coast of Maine. Sara's older daughter, Catherine, lives and works in nearby White Plains, New York. Her youngest daughter, Caroline, and her lawyer husband, John, keep a busy schedule overseeing their daughter and son in Charleston.

David's brother, Jack, died several years ago. His widow still resides in the family home in Walterboro, South Carolina, having retired many years ago from teaching English in the high school there. Their older daughter, BettyLlew, directs the gifted program for three counties, after having taught English in the local school for many years. Their younger daughter, Ann, lives in Davis, California, with her husband, Brian, and their two children, Catherine and Mat. Both parents are teachers at the University of California at Davis. Ann's younger brother, John, is a prominent lawyer in Columbia, South Carolina. He comes often to visit his mother and sister. Teaching seems to run in the family, as the daughter of BettyLlew and her husband, Steve, teaches in a private school.

Tom and I have always played guessing games when listening to classical music on the car radio when traveling. Since one of us knows the answer, it is always fun to see how long it takes the other to get the right answer. At the many concerts we attend, there is always a long discussion afterwards as to the pros and cons of the piece being played and/or the performance.

One of Tom's favorite hobbies is looking at someone's face and trying to guess in what country their ancestors lived. After all his travels, he gets the answer right most of the time.

Hearing different languages spoken keeps me entertained wherever I am. In airports, I relax while waiting for a departing flight and try to guess what language it is. I have discovered, however, that one hour's shopping at Walmart saves me the trouble of traveling!

Tom's two daughters are still living far from us. Cathy brings his grandchildren from Wisconsin to visit when their schedules allow. Coyote and his sister, Mayalee, are now in middle school, so it is hard to get together. Betsy is looking forward to owning her own house near Boston. Her work in a union office keeps her unavailable to visit here, but emails and phone calls keep us connected.

My eldest daughter, Sara, wanted to reclaim her childhood name of Michael so that her father's wish to have his first daughter named Michael will be honored.

Sara Michael, is still involved with the Friends School – the Quaker School in which she taught for ten years. Her 5' 5" tall, slim shape has never changed. On Fridays, she sits on the floor with her guitar, leading the four and five-year-olds in favorite songs. Her blue eyes shine under her light brown bangs as she draws each child's attention to the group's activity. Monday night singing lessons keep her clear voice strong. Chanting in San-skrit at her yoga meditation center is also a chance to sing. Her second husband, Rich, also plays guitar and sings. They provide entertainment at many of the gatherings they have at home and with friends.

In 1988, Sara Michael composed a whimsical poem for David entitled "Father's Day Brunch." It reads:

Everyone knows that words are important.
Everyone knows that words carry portent.
Everyone knows that the right word is crucial.
But no one ever cuts words out and floats them on ponds.
No one ever leads them on a string or eats them for lunch –
all in a
  bunch between the cheeses in great greasy chunks.
Why don't more take the hunch that words can be fun –
shhh!
  Crunch  crunch.


My favorite poem that Sara Michael wrote was the following:
  I heard God today.
  He said weave, weave and sing.
  Weave me a pattern of exquisite design.
  So I took the eyes of a butterfly wing
  And the mouth of a river
  And ears from the grain
  Weaving the face I saw
  With hair of sheep that still
  wander the valleys of shadow
  and know that they are loved.

The card she sent me on my seventieth birthday said, "Time may bring many changes to our lives, but through the years, some things last and grow even more precious – like the special joy of having you for a mom."

Her ex-husband, Chuck and his wife, Belle, with their two young sons, Sam and Andrew, live about five miles away. The two families get together for birthdays and holidays, whenever possible. Sara Michael and Chuck have remained best of friends since their divorce thirteen years ago.

Their daughter, Hannah, is a senior at the University of Georgia, where she is completing a degree in linguistics. In her spare time, she entertains herself and friends with her guitar.

Their younger son, Joseph, is studying computer science at Georgia Tech.

Kelli and her husband, Clif, are certainly an example of a couple where likes attract. Kelli, with her biology background, did cancer research for the National Institute of Health the year before they were married. Clif, with a background in chemistry, is still employed after twenty-seven years, by the American Dental Association as a research chemist. Their daughter, Lisa, is following in her parents' footsteps. After graduating from Johns Hopkins, she is now doing research for a consultant management company in Cambridge, Massachusetts. Their younger son, Clif, Junior, is majoring in engineering at Washington University in St. Louis, Missouri.

Kelli, my middle daughter, is following me in two ways. The nickname, Kelli, stands for Kellogg. Lisa, my granddaughter, is also Lisa Eleanor. The second way is traveling, as she accompanies Clif to the American Dental Association's annual conventions in Singapore, Sweden, and Paris, to name a few.

One Mother's Day, her card said "Wherever I am and whatever I do, there is one thing I always can count on from you – your love for me. And, however I change as years come and go, there's one thing I'm certain I'll never outgrow – my love for you."

My youngest daughter, Jennifer, now teaches learning-disabled sixth graders at a middle school near her home in Winder, Georgia. Her spare time includes walking her Chihuahua and miniature dachshund, as well as following the University of Georgia's football team's games with lively interest. Her son, David, graduated from the University of Georgia last May and is now employed as a policeman by Clarke County to work on the university's campus. Daniel is finishing his degree in computer science and serving faithfully with a campus ministry called

The Navigators at the same school. Dasha is a junior at Prince Avenue Christian School, a private school near Athens.

Thanks to our being only twenty minutes away from each other, we get together often to shop, eat out, or just talk about each other's concerns. On a recent occasion, she wrote, "I am so glad you're here through all these years. I'm glad we have been able to share in child-raising laughs and tears. You have put a song in my heart and unfailing optimism in my soul. You're not afraid to fly and you're not afraid to try new things. I know your prayers have kept me safe through my life, and for that I thank you. I love you because you are my mom!" At this backward glance at my three daughters, my heart does sing!

Malcolm came in and out of my life like a brightly colored strand of wool in a tartan from his Scottish heritage. Our first encounter was at David's fraternity house. Then he joined my college roommate, Mary Ann, in our wedding party to help us celebrate this happy occasion. David and Malcolm were classmates at seminary. In 1991, he and his lovely wife, Jacque, were our hosts when Tom and I attended my 50th high school reunion in Hartsville. The last time I saw Malcolm was six years later, when he came to the funeral of my older sister in Columbia, South Carolina.

My interest in people keeps me wondering who they are, where they come from, and what they are thinking. When I do get to know someone as I travel or meet them locally, their lives are meaningful. Friends I have made over the years have remained good friends – cards, phone calls, and emails keep us connected. The list includes college roommates, teacher associates, church members, and my neighbors not only at Iris Place, but in former towns. Ann, Winnie, and Rita are only an hour away in Atlanta. Billie and Peggy are living in different states. Betty and Dan started their friendship with David and me at seminary. Later on, we went sailing together. Now, after traveling the world together, we talk often about our joys and sorrows.

I sometimes think that I should add "keeping in touch" with people to my list of hobbies. Most people knit, collect coins, or enjoy gourmet cooking for a hobby. The time I spend at my desk or computer gives me great pleasure.

My older sister, Connie, died three years ago. I will always miss her thoughtful comments on some far-out scheme I was considering. At the time of her death, she was still walking two miles before breakfast, joining the water aerobics class at the YWCA, and working with CORE of the Small Business Administration. Here she taught a business course for young men who were first offenders at the local prison.

Connie lived with her only daughter, Gay, and her husband, Jeff. Their daughter, Anna Caroline, works as a counselor at the Lexington-Richland Alcohol and Drug Abuse Clinic in Columbia. Their son, Billy, is an outstanding athlete and student in his junior year at a private school in town. Her oldest brother, Michael, is a day trader in Colorado. Steve, the next brother in line, is an outstanding pulmonary specialist in California. Another younger brother, Robert, is a top orthopedic specialist in Charleston, South Carolina, and her youngest brother, Pat, is a career Army counselor for alcohol and drug addiction in Texas. They really have an interesting time at family reunions!

My younger sister, Mary Rice, whose name we have shortened to Ricie, lives with her husband, Jim, in Summerville, South Carolina, where they can be near the family of one of their six sons. During the time her husband was a Presbyterian minister in a small West Virginia coal mine town, Ricie chose to home school her sons. A visiting VISTA worker could see the academic potential in these boys and suggested having them tested at Phillips Exeter Academy in Massachusetts. They tested so high that four of the boys attended this fine boy's school from seventh grade until they graduated. A fifth one graduated from Woodbury Forest in Virginia. At present, the eldest, Ed, and his family are missionaries in Morelos, Mexico, where he trains Mexicans to be missionaries in Mexico. Their second son, Scott, graduated from Harvard Law School and was head of the Home School Legal Defense. The next son, Jim, Jr., has his doctorate of theology, and after serving a Baptist church several blocks from the White House for seven years, has recently become the senior minister of the First Baptist Church in Richmond, Virginia, where his Sunday morning service is televised. A fourth son, Greg, has just become a minister in a thriving church in Gaithersburg, Maryland. His younger brother, Grey, is self employed in telecommunications. And the sixth son, Bill, has just started working on a doctorate in psychology in New York City. This certainly tells me a lot about home schooling! In addition they had parents who believed in cultivating their individual passions and skills.

When they were living near me in Arden, North Carolina, Ricie satisfied some of her longings for daughters by writing a monthly news letter entitled, "Dear Daughters." She is a real "pack rat" and had files full of ways to fix hamburger, hints on how to grow vegetables and flowers, and general good advice a mother would want to give to make a daughter's life easier. I subscribed to this letter for most of the ten years she wrote it. At the end of the ten years, Ricie had nearly one hundred on her mailing list of friends and their friends!

My brother, Evans, who is five years younger than Ricie, changed his name to "E.K." when he attended Davidson College. He got tired of explaining that there was an "s" on the end of his name. Inheriting the boundless energy that gets me in so much trouble, he is motion personified. Twenty years ago he married a second time to a wonderful woman, who is fifteen years younger. Marianne has enjoyed keeping up with him, as he sets goals such as climbing every mountain over ten thousand feet west of the Mississippi River.

His older daughter, Kim, and her husband, Jeff, ride herd on our family's only set of twins, Ben and Izzy, in Tulsa, Oklahoma. They attend a preschool in which Spanish is the only language spoken. In addition, Kim is the author of two books and spends every chance she gets creating computer art which she puts on cards and posters. Her younger brother, Scott, applauds his sister's creativity from his home in Houston, Texas.

My youngest sister, Anna Belle, was born as we were leaving home for college and marriage. She inherited our Aunt Caroline's artistic ability and has spent most of her sixty-four years using these talents. Her 5' 8" sturdy frame was put to good use, when she was recently installed ten-foot bamboo arches at an outdoor sculpture exhibit. Her daughter, Sia, lives in CA. Her name is short for Anastasia. She has a slim, diminutive figure and a beautiful heart shaped face reflecting her father's Russian heritage.

Living in Lynn, Massachusetts, Anna Belle passes the historical cemetery where our ancestor, the Rev. Samuel Whiting, is buried. Over the years, Anna Belle has generously shared many of her creations with me.

We all have been grateful to our mother for instilling in us healthy eating habits. I grieve when I think of how I could not thank our mother before she died. I hope she can see our vitality and youthful appearances. During a phone call recently, the information that I was seventy-eight was unbelievable to the caller. "You certainly don't sound like you are that old," she exclaimed.

Our parent's love of the outdoors is another gift we inherited. We would visit our Whiting grandparent's estate in Shulls Mills, North Carolina, in the summer time. My grandfather, who was a lumberman, would delight in identifying different trees in their large yard. He would break off a branch so that we could smell the different woods and then point out the difference in leaf shapes. Today, on my art table, I have a design of yellow gingko leaves waiting for my water color brush to duplicate.

When it seems that life is "upside down and backwards" and I can't see how a problem with time or events can possibly be resolved, I get an inner calm assurance that all will be well. It is like the resettling of the yellow, blue, red and green balls in a gum ball machine. One question I will want to ask when I get to eternity is, "Is this optimism?" One fact I do not question is the persistence and ingenuity, and curiosity that I inherited from my parents. These attributes have opened many doors for me that, without them, would have remained shut.

My journey in faith started in my youth. Through the years, events in my life have tested it been made stronger. I am a member of the Bell Choir at Friendship Presbyterian Church. The resonating tone of the large brass hand bell, as it makes the circular swing in front of me, gives me "goose bumps!"

When my name was submitted for the position of ruling elder this summer, I was deeply honored and have accepted this role. During my three-year term, I hope to make a significant contribution to the life of this very vital church. When I begin each day with personal devotions, I am thankful for family and friends who have encouraged my spiritual journey.

Music has been the greatest joy in my life. Playing a musical instrument and/or singing most of my life, I continue to appreciate music at every opportunity. Music must be handed down from generation to generation, as my daughters play the guitar and sing. For my seventy-eighth birthday this summer, Sara Michael presented me with a tape of the twenty-third psalm from the Bible's Old Testament. On this tape she composed music to accompany the Hebrew text of this psalm. Daniel, one of my grandchildren, plays the guitar and banjo. He also has written the gospel blue grass music on two of three CDs which he has recorded. Beginning when he was eleven, he continues to play with The Threads of Hope, a gospel blue grass group from Winder, as a senior at the University of Georgia. His younger sister, Dasha, is looking for a drum teacher to improve her performance with her church group.

C.J., another grandson, took drum lessons for six years and also learned to play hand bells in his church choir. He continues both of these on his college campus. His older sister, Lisa, sang solo and in group performances during her high school and college years. How I wish I could live to see what the NEXT generation will produce!

Michael H. Lindvall, pastor of the Brick Presbyterian Church in New York City, once said "The road is the teacher!" This struck a strong chord in me as I look back on the lessons I have learned. The result of these lessons is a very full life. When I see this full life reflected in my daughter's lives, my "cup" overflows. All my life, my heart has been blessed with the sound of music – and so I look forward to the years ahead – with a song in my heart.

# ELEANOR KELLOGG WHITING MOYLAN GENEALOGY

Some of my children, grandchildren or great-grandchildren may want to do genealogical research for a more complete account of their ancestors. Below is a partial history to show them how rich their heritage is. It is only a start, as they can find a wealth of information about their lineage and each individual listed below on the computer and in genealogical sections of libraries. Few families are fortunate as ours to have had as many distinguished ancestors. Our Parmalee family was part of the New Haven colonial elite. John Parmalee lived where the First Congregational Church centers on the New Haven Green in Connecticut. Our Kellogg line can be traced back to William the Conqueror and royal families of Britain and France.

As an aid to descendants who wish to trace our ancestry, here is a brief directory to help begin the search:

WHITING LINE

Eleanor Kellogg Whiting (born 1931) is the daughter of William Scott Whiting, Jr. and Emily Mather Kellogg.

William Scott Whiting, Jr. (born 1907) was the son of William Scott Whiting, Sr.

William Scott Whiting, Sr. (born 1871) was the son of Henry Whiting.

Henry Whiting (born 1818) was the son of John Whiting.

John Whiting (born 1782) was the seventh generation grandson of The Rev. Samuel Whiting of Lynn, Massachusetts.

## KELLOGG LINE

Emily Mather Kellogg (born 1907) was the daughter of Evans Shipman Kellogg and Cornelia Helen Mather.

Evans Shipman Kellogg (born 1876) was the son of William Parmalee Kellogg and Frances Amelia Parmalee.

William Parmalee Kellogg (born 1837) was the son of Charles Harvey Kellogg and Frances Amelia Parmalee.

Charles Harvey Kellogg (born 1808) was the son of Charles Harvey Kellogg and Mary Ann Otis.

Charles Harvey Kellogg (born 1773) was the son of Asa Kellogg and Lucy Powell.

## MATHER LINE

Cornelia Helen Mather (born 1873) was the daughter of Frederick Gregory Mather and Cornelia Heyer Olcott.

Frederick Gregory Mather (born 1844) was the son of Samuel Holmes Mather and Emily Worthington Gregory.

Samuel Holmes Mather (born 1813) was the son of Ozias

Mather and Harriett Brainard.

## PARMALEE LINE

Frances Amelia Parmalee (born 1811) was the daughter of Elias Parmalee and Fanny Fitch.

Elias Parmalee (born 1774) was the son of Hezekiah Parmalee, Jr. (born 1737) and Elizabeth Cook.

Manufactured By:    RR Donnelley
Breinigsville, PA USA
June, 2010